# COMPETITION IS IRRELEVANT

## The Essential Workbook for Creating a Stand-Out Brand

**Peg Marckworth**

SILVER FERN
PUBLISHING

Marckworth, Peg.

Competition is irrelevant: the essential workbook for creating a stand-out brand
Print: 978-0-9961553-0-4
E-book: 978-0-9961553-1-1
Library of Congress Control Number: 2015903668

Printed in the United States of America

1. Branding    2. Marketing    3. Entrepreneurship    4. Small Business

Cover and text design by Leslie Waltzer, Crowfoot Design (www.crowfootdesign.com)
Author photo by Landin Williams (www.landinwilliams.com)

Silver Fern Publishing
6837 29th Avenue Northeast
Seattle, WA 98115
USA
www.silverfernpublishing.com

While the author has made every effort to provide accurate Internet addresses at the time of publication, neither the publisher nor the author assumes any responsibility for errors or for changes that occur after publication. Further, the publisher does not have any control over and does not assume any responsibility for author or third party Websites or their content.

Although every precaution has been taken to verify the accuracy of the information contained herein, the author and publisher assume no responsibility for any errors or omissions. No liability is assumed for damages that may result from the use of information contained within.

Silver Fern Publishing books are available at special quantity discounts to use for educational, business or promotional use. For information, please email info@silverfernpublishing.com.

# TABLE OF CONTENTS

# FOREWORD
## Christopher Flett

Over seventeen years ago, as a recent university graduate, I was hired for my first 'branding' job at a public utility company. On the first day of training, the Marketing Vice President told us 'branding' was like 'branding cattle'; we were to get our programs into the minds of our customers by ensuring our logo was on everything. We had to bring up the name of our company, share our mission statement, and get our logo in front of them (normally in the form of a balloon handed to their kid, an instant tattoo, or some cheap swag for them to take home—usually a 'reusable bag').

For years and years, I had it in my mind, that branding was simply using your logo to build recognition in the market. Even the branding professionals I came across focused me on choosing a color palate, a visual logo and a mission statement that was supposed to guide me.

What I didn't realize was that the branding definitions they had shared with me weren't a component of brand; they were a mere hint of brand. What was sold to me as the whole kit and caboodle was not even one percent of the conversation. As the years have gone on, branding has come further and further into the forefront and now seems to be the core of all conversations around business development. Yet the story still seemed to just touch on the topic rather that getting deep into the conversation on not only what brand is, but how to use it properly. And so I, like many, continued to feel my way through the conversation just picking up pieces, trying to put the puzzle together. More confusing still was that these pieces often contradicted each other.

Then in 2011 I met Peg Marckworth and within minutes of having a coffee with her, realized that she had sorted out not only what all the pieces were in the branding equation, but how they went together and how to use them. Not only did it fill in the many gaps in the subject that I had, but put a spotlight on how much I didn't know. Before Peg, I didn't know what I didn't know. Spending time with her, I began to know what I didn't know. Then putting her information into practice, I began to 'own' the knowledge both in theory and application (knowing what I know) and hope to move to the point where all my decisions around my business models have an automatic consideration of brand in my thinking process.

*Competition is Irrelevant* is the book I wish I had received on the first day at that first job. It perfectly marries the theory of Branding, describes what it entails and shows how to apply those pieces in ways that gets measurable results. Brand has been sidelined for too many years by design, but as you start to wield it as a business development tool, you realize that while it offers qualitative results on your business, it also offers quantitative results to your bottom line. Why be a cola when you can be Coke?

This book has the ability to expedite your conversations about brand into tactics and measurable results that will benefit your business and your bottom line. By the time you are finished, you will have completed in mere hours that which I struggled with for over a decade and a half. Knowledge is power and *Competition is Irrelevant* is a welcome (and in my opinion...long overdue) addition to any professional's technical tool box. Finally the conversation surrounding brand has guidance and a calibration point. Read it once, and then revisit it and work through the tasks, then work it again and again as you distill down the brand model of your business. Write in the columns, highlight passages, stuff it with sticky notes, and make it yours. The harder your book looks worked, the stronger your bottom line will become.

- **Christopher V. Flett**

    Author of *What Men Don't Tell Women About Business—
    Opening Up the Heavily Guarded Alpha Male Playbook* and
    *Market Shark: How To Be a Big Fish In a Small Pond*

    Founder of Ghost CEO™ and Chairman of Flett Ventures Inc.

CHAPTER 1

# WHAT IS A BRAND AND WHY DO YOU NEED ONE?
## An Introduction to Branding

## I 'DISCOVERED' THE REAL MEANING OF BRANDING IN 2003

The PR firm I co-owned in the early 2000s promoted small businesses across the U.S. and Canada. I'd known for a long time that we were able to get the best results when our clients had a compelling story to tell—those stories were the basis for good PR. I hadn't yet learned that the best stories came from clients who understood who they were and what was unique about them. When our clients made a promise through their story and then fulfilled that promise through every interaction they had with media, customers and the public—we had a winner and the media loved it. I didn't yet realize that this was a strong brand at work.

In 2003 I picked up the book *Brand Driven* by F. Joseph LePla, Susan V. Davis and Lynn M. Parker and read:

> *Many leaders mistakenly believe brand is a marketing problem, reserved for those c ompanies that can afford Super Bowl ads or snazzy logos. But a brand is the sum total of every experience a customer has with a company or product—a sum total that customers begin to think of as the promise of the brand. The reality is if you want to create a strong brand, keeping the brand promise is every leader's responsibility. Brand value and customer loyalty come from smart and disciplined leaders who implement brand strategy and model brand action every day.* [1]

The concepts of brand and branding were hardly new in 2003 but the idea of integrated branding—a brand built on company strengths and what customers value—and implemented across the company—was a new concept to me and I immediately embraced it.

The worst outcome of a 'great' media story is when consumers realize that it's an empty story—all spin with an unfulfilled promise. Our firm wanted success for our clients beyond the quantity of media coverage. We wanted consumers to embrace the company, person or product. I realized that this meant developing integrated brand strategy for these clients. I read and learned all I could so I could teach my PR clients how fully integrating their brand into their business could help them succeed.

Since 2003, Brand Strategy for professionals and small businesses has been the primary focus of my work. I teach clients how to integrate their brand into their business by knowing who they are, what they promise and how to fulfill that promise in every interaction.

I believe in branding. I'm a brand evangelist. I want every professional and business owner to understand their brand and recognize its power. A brand gives you a sustainable identity: solid at its core but flexible and responsive enough to evolve. Your business will most effectively serve the needs of your target market with a strong brand to guide it. A strong brand frees you to do what you love and build a business that makes you proud.

Every business and every professional has a brand. It's not a poetic idea created and draped over a business. It's not a marketing tactic. It's who you are, what you do and how you benefit those you most want to serve.

Developing a strong brand that supports your business is a process of discovery that unveils what makes you unique, memorable, believable and important to your target audience. It supports you in making good business decisions, structures your communication, and keeps you focused and strong. Understanding your brand promise allows you to express it fully and keeps you focused on fulfilling it in every interaction you have with customers. Your brand keeps you on track to succeed.

This book is a step-by-step guide for developing an integrated brand specifically for your business or career. Working through the chapters will allow you to reveal the strongest and best parts of who you are and what you offer clients. It will give you a framework and the vocabulary to talk about what makes you and your brand truly unique. As a result you will communicate more effectively with the clients you want to work with and they, in turn, will recognize your value to them.

## BEFORE WE BEGIN TALKING ABOUT WHAT A BRAND IS, WE NEED TO PUT BRAND INTO CONTEXT

### BRAND TERMINOLOGY

Today, I hear "brand" and "branding" everywhere I go. These terms are applied to products, services, companies, individuals, non-profits, government initiatives, sports teams, political parties, cities, states, countries and more. But no one seems to know what they really mean.

I can't count the number of times I've been at networking events with graphic designers, web designers, public relations and marketing consultants, advertising folks, photographers, or fashion stylists who say: "I brand my clients." Each person knows what they mean and each one has a useful, sometimes critical, role in helping individuals and businesses stand out from their competition. But the person they are talking to—who might be a prospective client—is often completely lost.

Brand jargon can be overwhelming. This word cloud shows just some of the terms used to talk about or explain brands and branding. Is it any wonder we're confused?

## THE TOP 5 BRANDING MISSTEPS

To understand the strengths of integrated branding and to prepare you to build your own brand we need first to look at some branding missteps. These confusions almost always are related to jumping into action before you have developed your brand strategy.

Identifying these missteps will give you better insight about integrated branding and prepare you to develop a strong brand for yourself.

## MISSTEP #1: BRANDING IS SEEN AS BEING THE SAME THINGS AS MARKETING

Nothing could be further from the truth. Branding is integral to marketing but you can't market well until you understand and can communicate your brand.

In the simplest terms, branding is strategic and marketing is tactical. You need both.

Brand strategy is the process of identifying the most compelling and unique things about you and combining them into a promise that is both communicated and fulfilled. It defines the specific solution you have to the specific problem of a specific set of customers.

Branding lets you stand out from your competition. It's relevant and credible and truthful. It gives you information that allows you to make and keep an emotional connection with customers. It is the foundation for successful marketing.

Marketing is the set of tactics you use to promote your product, service or business. Marketing campaigns are the vehicles for connecting to your target audience, generating leads and sales and to positioning your brand. Marketing consists of a coordinated set of steps, designed to build your brand image, introduce a new product or service, increase sales of an existing product or service or reduce the impact of negative publicity. Marketing campaigns utilize media outreach, public relations, word-of-mouth, social media, events and advertising.

Successful marketing campaigns support your brand strategy and messages.

In 2012 Pepsi launched a major reevaluation of its brand based on the realization that its marketing strategies were not grounded in a clear brand strategy. In a 9-month global campaign to discover what made it unique (which largely meant different from Coke), Pepsi conducted "focus groups, in-home ethnographies, quantitative and qualitative studies, and cultural immersions in markets as diverse as Argentina, Australia, United Arab Emirates and Russia." It found consistencies in who it was perceived to be, both historically and culturally.

> "Coke," Mr. Jakeman said [Brad Jakeman, President-Global Enjoyment and Chief Creative Officer], "represents happiness and moments of joy, while it protects culture and maintains the status quo. Pepsi, on the other hand, creates culture and embraces individuality. For Pepsi loyalists, leading an exciting life is much more important than leading a happy one.
>
> Those insights led Pepsi to embrace a brand positioning to 'capture the excitement of now,' and the campaign that has been developed carries the tagline, 'Live for Now.' It's already proved a potent rallying cry. [2]

Today, Pepsi's marketing is driven by its brand and focuses on staying on the cutting edge of popular culture. An example of this is Pepsi Pulse, the official website of the cola brand (www.pepsipulse.com). The website focuses on entertainment, sports and music of interest of Millennials, its primary target market.

## MISSTEP #2: PEOPLE DON'T UNDERSTAND BRAND STRATEGY

The term "branding" is ubiquitous. But, as the word cloud on page 3 shows, what branding means is unclear at best.

People often say: "I have a logo and website, so I have a brand, don't I?" Unfortunately, the answer is "no." Your brand is not a logo, tag line or website. These are tools that communicate your brand. They're important—very important—because they catch people's attention, connect with them emotionally and remind them who you are.

But branding isn't something you add to a product or service before you send it to market. A true brand says what you're going to do. If what you say through your brand and what you deliver are disconnected you've lost the opportunity to develop and keep a relationship with your customer.

Branding doesn't work when it's superficial and disconnected from the person, product or service it's intended to showcase. When it's layered on top rather than coming from within, it fails. It's easy to spend a lot of money and time on marketing campaigns that have nothing to do with your heart and soul—your brand. This can be a costly mistake.

Brand strategy is taking the time to know yourself and what you offer. It means knowing your target audience and what they want and need. It means building a relationship with your customer that is based on trust and delivers what you promise. It means that every time your customer interacts with you they get what they expect and that increases the likelihood that they will return again and again.

This is brand strategy. It is the foundation that informs all your marketing and communications. It's a tool to help you make good business decisions, communicate effectively and keep your promise to the marketplace. Brand strategy starts with knowing what you promise and then fulfilling that promise with every interaction. Many people and companies don't have their brand strategy in place before they start selling their products/services. The ones who do can weather difficult times.

Customers change what they want and need. Brands must adapt to stay relevant. Brand strategy facilitates adaptation that remains true to the core brand and the target audience.

Here's a company that's taking the right steps. McDonald's is drawing on its core brand strategy to weather a difficult time for the company. McDonald's is still the largest fast-food chain in the U.S but between 2011 and the end of 2014 their market share, especially among Millennials, dropped significantly. This important market segment prefers healthier and fresher ingredients—and customization of their meal. [3]

In a January 2015 press release McDonald's wrote: "McDonald's legacy was built on providing special moments for families. Today we're working harder than ever to evolve with our customers. We're moving from a philosophy of, 'billions served' to 'billions heard.'" [4]

In a WARC news article on January 27, 2015, Mike Andres, president of McDonald's USA, said that McDonald's "is offering greater personalization through the Create Your Taste platform being rolled out in the US and Australia." CEO Don Thompson felt this "has the potential to lift sales of core classics, by bringing more customers into our restaurants." Create Your Taste, Thompson declared, "is a much broader piece than simply about the food itself. It is about the overall experience." [5]

## MISSTEP #3: PEOPLE (AND COMPANIES) DON'T KNOW HOW THEY ARE DIFFERENT FROM OTHERS

In order to choose you—and keep coming back—your customers need to know who you are, what you do and why you are the right choice for them. Whether you're building a business or a career, brand strategy gives you focus, differentiates your message and makes you stand out in an authentic and sustainable way.

If your brand is not based on strategy you can fall into a number of traps. There are a number of common things people and companies say to convince clients to choose them:

- I'm excellent—I have great customer service
- I can do whatever you need—I can do that…
- I have the cheapest price in town

It's important to avoid these traps.

### I'M EXCELLENT. I HAVE GREAT CUSTOMER SERVICE

Being great at what you do isn't enough. Prospective customers need to understand why you are right for them by understanding: who you are, what you offer and what differentiates you from your competitors.

Professionals spend years gaining the education and experience to call themselves experts. This process represents many hours and many dollars invested. From the inside looking out this education and experience seem significant and important. However, for the clients of these professionals, excellence is a baseline. It's a starting point. No one wants a "pretty-good" lawyer, an "average" accountant or an "OK" surgeon. We want the best. Only then do we look for other characteristics that indicate the professional will be a good fit for us.

Imagine you are a first time homebuyer. You feel excited, nervous and a little overwhelmed. You want a real estate agent you can depend on who knows the market, will understand you and what you want and need. You research agents and find three who have consistently excellent results and equal experience. You interview all three.

The first agent specializes in the neighborhood you want to live in. She knows the history of the houses on the market and has sold some of them over the years—some more than once. She has lived in the neighborhood for years and gives you "insider" information on the best areas, shops, services, schools, parks and recreational opportunities.

The second agent knows the market trends and is able to give you a current market assessment in a way that you can understand. She shares charts, graphs and data that explain the market assessment clearly and concisely. She's quick and efficient but makes sure you understand each point before she moves on.

The third agent really listens to you. Not only that, she helps you understand what features of a home and neighborhood are important to you. She recognizes how nervous you are and promises to walk you through each step, taking as much time as you need. She's a bit like your mom—and she brings cookies.

All have equal experience and success rates. One is not better than the others, but one is a better fit for you. You may not have known what you were looking for but you recognize which one is right for you.


**I CAN DO WHATEVER YOU NEED. I CAN DO THAT...**

It's a common mistake to think that offering more products and services to more people will bring you more business. It seems logical that the wider you cast your net the more successful you will be. In fact, the opposite is true.

Narrowing your target market to a specific niche allows you to meet the exact needs of those clients. Working with a specific and narrow group increases the "match" between you and them. When you work with "X group" it's your specialty. Your experience is with this group so you know it inside and out. You network in places where members of this group hang out. You gain credibility and flexibility within this niche market and before long you are the expert and the logical choice for this customer.

Enterprise Rent-A-Car is a great example of the power of tightening your niche market. Most rental car companies target travelers, especially business travelers. For their customers' convenience they locate their offices at airports and other travel-friendly locations. Enterprise Rent-A-Car saw an opportunity to offer customer service to another group of customers in need of rental cars. The company targets customers who need a car because their car was stolen or is in the shop, use public transportation to commute to work and want a car for only for events or trips, or are a one-car family who needs a second car for a short time.

To meet the needs of this customer Enterprise Rent-A-Car focuses on three unique strategies:

1. They have offices within 15 miles of 90% of the U.S. population. These offices are in neighborhoods and city locations that are convenient to customers.[6]

2. They pick you up, without fee—at your house or your office or your auto repair shop—and take you to their office to pick up your rental car. This customer service offers a convenience other rental car companies don't provide. It is a key differentiator.[7]

3. They partner with auto repair shops and insurance companies to provide rental cars to their customers. These partner companies are then able to recommend a convenient service to their customers that benefits them as well.[8]

Enterprise Rent-A-Car, built around a niche market, is now the largest rental car company in the U.S.[9]

## I HAVE THE CHEAPEST PRICE IN TOWN

A common strategy is to think and say: "I'm just like my competition—only cheaper."

When you try to set yourself apart on the basis of price you indicate that your product or service has little value other than its cheapness.

If the only difference between you and your competition is price then you've set yourself up to lose customers. Your customer will go to your competition when they offer a lower price or have a sale. They will "shop around." You won't be unique in their minds and they won't believe you offer them anything they can't get somewhere else.

The only one who can successfully compete on price is the one who can afford to offer the lowest price. There is a reason the biggest chain stores, like Walmart have the lowest prices: size, efficiency and economy of scale. Very few professionals and small business owners compete on price alone. You need to offer something that is worth a higher price.

Nordstrom (although by no means a small business) is a prime example of this. I ask my workshop participants: "What do you think of when I say Nordstrom?" One hundred percent of the time people say: "Customer service!"

What Nordstrom offers is beyond price. The Nordstrom culture supports and encourages each employee to look for opportunities to give you, the customer, the "Nordstrom experience." They don't want you to shop for something to wear—they want you to be a "Nordstrom shopper." They describe themselves on the About Us page of their website:

> *An unerring eye for what's next in fashion. A relentless drive to exceed expectations. For more than 100 years, Nordstrom has worked to deliver the best possible shopping experience, helping customers possess style—not just buy fashion.*
>
> *Nordstrom, Inc. is a leading fashion specialty retailer offering compelling clothing, shoes and accessories for men, women and children. Since 1901, we've been committed to providing our customers with the best possible service—and to improving it every day.*[10]

In *Leave It Better Than You Found It*, Bruce A. Nordstrom discussed the company's commitment to service:

> *We pride ourselves on our reputation for customer service, which goes all the way back to my grandpa's day. Some people may think that the idea for giving good service suddenly came to us in a flash of light, but that was not the case. Our reputation for service is the result of an evolutionary process that spans the history of our company. Why have we emphasized service? It is very simple. Over the years, we learned that the more service we provided, the better our business became. It's no more complicated than that.*[11]
>
> *To us, service is the honorable thing. Service is about elevating the person you are waiting on, making the person feel better about the shopping experience. We understand completely that our customers are deserving of kindness, attention, and professionalism.*[12]

## MISSTEP #4: PEOPLE LET THE MARKET DEFINE THEM

If your brand isn't clear, the market decides who you are—and they may not get it right.

Jeff Bezos, Founder of Amazon, said once: *"Your brand is what people say about you when you're not in the room."* Your brand lives in the hearts and minds of customers, clients and prospects. It is the sum of their experiences and perceptions.

How the market perceives your brand is fluid and based on both tangible and intangible aspects of what you offer. It includes the experience people have with you but also what they hear about from other people, online and through social media.

According to Tim Ferriss, author of *The 4-Hour Workweek*, "Personal branding is about managing your name—even if you don't own a business—in a world of misinformation, disinformation, and semi-permanent Google records. Going on a date? Chances are that your "blind" date has Googled your name. Going to a job interview? Ditto."[13]

For the market to understand what you offer and how it benefits them two key things come into play: being clear about what you promise and doing what you say you will do.

It's easy to say you do this and hard to do it well. The process needs to be deliberate, well planned and consistent. Many professionals and small businesses overlook this important first step.

FedEx built its business on the promise of reliability. What they do to fulfill that promise has evolved as the industry has evolved. When the company started in the early 1980s, they promised to deliver packages by 10:30 the next day—and they did. Their success at fulfilling their promise changed their industry. Their competition—including the U.S. Postal Service—began successfully delivering packages overnight so this no longer set them apart. They developed a tracking service so their customers could have "peace of mind" about where their packages were—which again set them apart. Once again, their competitors followed their lead. (Imitation is the sincerest form of flattery.) FedEx's acquisition of Kinko's (now FedEx Office) expanded their service offerings but did not change their promise of reliability. FedEx understands their promise and delivers on that promise even as their industry changes and they offer new products and services.

## MISSTEP #5: BRANDING IS SEEN AS A COST NOT AN INVESTMENT

Small businesses and professionals must pay attention to their bottom line in order to stay in business. Cutting costs and maintaining cash flow are daily issues. Many business costs—facility, labor and inventory—are not optional. So the idea of paying for, much less financing, the cost of branding can seem unthinkable. I've heard business owners say:

- Branding would be great, but I just can't afford it.
- I need a website—brochure—business cards—more right now.
- I'll just get a logo.
- My nephew/intern/neighbor can build me a website.
- Not branding won't make that much difference.

A more important question is: "What is the cost of not branding my business?"

Unfortunately there are real costs that come from a failure to develop your brand. They fall into four categories: money, time, energy and reputation.

## WASTING YOUR MONEY

**Spending your marketing dollars on campaigns that don't work is a cost you cannot afford.**

## WASTING YOUR TIME

If you are reaching out to target customers in the wrong ways you are spending time you could use more effectively.

## THE EMOTIONAL COST

You know you have something great to offer but you can't seem to reach the right people. You and your staff risk frustration and burn-out.

## LOSING CONTROL OF YOUR REPUTATION

Marketing communication that isn't rooted in Brand Strategy can do more harm than good.

Letting your competition get ahead. If you aren't speaking to the right people in the right places with the right messages you leave room for your competition to be there instead—gaining visibility and credibility that leaves you as an "also ran."

Losing potential clients. When prospects don't understand what you offer, are under-whelmed by your messages or define you in ways that may not be true they quickly turn away. You may never be able to get their attention again.

Not branding is like deciding not to register the title on your car—you may think you own it, but you don't. You still have to make car payments, buy fuel and maintain it but it's really not yours.

# THE HISTORY OF BRANDING

People have marked their products as long as goods have been sold or traded. A marked product was recognizable no matter where it travelled. A maker's mark denoted a certain level of quality. People would seek out marked products to be assured of quality.

The term "brand" derives from the Old Norse word *brandr* meaning 'to burn'. A brand burned with a hot iron showed ownership of property. Cattle were branded so that no matter where they wandered their ownership was legally acknowledged. People were branded for a variety of reasons. Slaves were branded to show ownership. Criminals were branded to shame them. Prisoners in Nazi concentration camps were tattooed with numbers or forced to wear symbols on their clothing to show they were not equal.

The industrial revolution brought mass production and predictable quality. Production methods guaranteed standardization of products so quality stopped being the primary differentiator.

By the early 20th century the U. S. was prosperous enough to support a consumer economy. People with disposable income spent it on brand name items: automobiles, radios and phonographs, beverages and cigarettes. Brand name goods were seen as special and desirable—beyond their quality. Consumers could enhance their image by using these brands. They were marketed on their ability to give the consumer prestige. In many cases image enhancement was more important to the consumer than the functionality of the item.

By the middle of the 20th century brand name products flourished in the post-war consumer economy. Kellogg's cereals, Coca Cola—and Pepsi—Copper Tone, Kodak, Pillsbury, Marlboro and many car brands developed advertising campaigns designed to connect emotionally with their customers. Consumers wanted a modern lifestyle and brand name products offered to provide it.

This was the era of Madison Avenue advertising agencies (think *Mad Men*—the TV series about Madison Avenue Advertising firms in the 1960s). These agencies built relationships between products and consumers through advertising and their goal was to make these relationships last a lifetime. Manufacturers learned to build their product's identity through its personality by giving it human characteristics: fun, youthful, honest, friendly, adventurous, or brave. The objective was for consumers to buy "the brand" not just the product.

Marketers gave products identities that were unique when compared to other similar products. Consumers learned to look for brand name products when they shopped: Kellogg's Corn Flakes, Coca Cola (or Pepsi) soda, Heinz ketchup and Tide detergent. Customers became fiercely loyal to these products even if they couldn't identify them in blind taste tests. These brands made the promise that they were special and the consumer was special when they used them. But what they promised was often an illusion. Smoking Marlboro cigarettes didn't make you the Marlboro man.

Brands interacted with consumers primarily through advertising that informed through carefully crafted messages. Ad agencies used focus groups to understand what consumers wanted. Yet, while building the brand was important, the primary focus of every strong manufacturer remained the production of goods.

The shift from production to a focus on brand grew over a quarter century until by the early 1970s the focus of large corporations was producing brands rather than products. Advertising campaigns were designed to fulfill the emotional and social needs of consumers as much or more than their product needs.

Naomi Klein in her book, *No Logo: Taking Aim at the Brand Bullies* writes:

> *At around this same time a new kind of corporation began to rival the traditional all-American manufacturers for market share; these were the Nikes and Microsofts, and later, the Tommy Hilfigers and Intels. These pioneers made the bold claim that producing goods was only an incidental part of their operations, and that thanks to recent victories in trade liberalization and labor-law reform, they were able to have their products made for them by contractors, many of them overseas. What these companies produced primarily were not things, they said, but images of their brands. Their real work lay not in manufacturing but in marketing. This formula, needless to say, has proved enormously profitable, and its success has companies competing in a race toward weightlessness: whoever owns the least, has the fewest employees on the payroll and produces the most powerful images, as opposed to products, wins the race.*[14]

Branding was dealt a serious blow on April 2, 1993 when Philip Morris announced they were cutting the price of Marlboro cigarettes (one of the most iconic brands of the 20th century) by 20% to complete with bargain brands.[15] Their decision to compete on price rather than image popped the image branding balloon. Wall Street responded dramatically with stock prices nose-diving for a large number of companies selling branded products, including Tide, Quaker Oats, Heinz, and Pepsi.

Although this event was shocking, it was part of a larger trend. The recession in the late 1970s and early 1980's created a subtle change in attitudes toward brands. In the 1980s, people's brand loyalty was increasingly displaced by the desire for 'brand value'. Consumers wanted lower prices and were willing to look for them in products without logos and big advertising programs. Consumers looked for "store brands" that often had reduced labeling and packaging. They were "no-frills" and lower in price.

The 1980s and 1990s also saw the rapid growth of "Big Box" stores like Walmart, Kmart and Target, and "Club Stores" like Costco and Sam's Club. They epitomized the public's desire for bargains and value.

Interestingly, despite this price-focused market with consumers looking for cost over brand, a small subset of brands grew. They were brands that offered lifestyle beyond their product. Two prime corporate examples of this are Calvin Klein and Nike.

- Calvin Klein changed jeans in the late 1970s by putting his name on the back pocket and featuring them in his designer fashion shows. The Calvin Klein brand quickly became synonymous with the young urban professional lifestyle. By the early 1980s Calvin Klein solidified its role as a lifestyle brand with Brooke Shields, Marky Mark (Mark Wahlberg) and Kate Moss featured in its jeans ads and the tagline "Nothing comes between me and my Calvins." Building on this success Calvin Klein introduced a line of men's underwear. The advertising campaign featuring celebrity models, including Antonio Sabato Jr., Mark Wahlberg, Swedish soccer star Freddie Ljungberg and Justin Bieber, has spanned 30 years.

- Nike unrolled its tagline "Just Do It" in 1988[16] to represent its promise to "bring inspiration and innovation to every athlete in the world."[17] Whether you jogged in the neighborhood, reached for the Olympics or were a professional athlete, Nike promised to partner with you, inspiring you to reach your highest potential. It continues this promise today.

Branding saw a resurgence in the late 1990s as the focus of companies moved from product to brand as the best route to profits. Consumers still wanted value and price in many things; they saved money on economy brands as a way to purchase brands they saw as essential to their lifestyle.

Jack Myers wrote in his 1993 book, *Adbashing: Surviving the Attacks on Advertising*:

> In the 1990s, consumers are becoming far more discriminating. Purchases are less conspicuous and far more considered. Society, like the tectonic plates in California, is shifting and resettling into new configurations. Marketers are hoping that the shifts are completed and consumers will settle into a new set of comfortable, somewhat traditional patterns. But more than likely, the shifts are an early warning sign that far more cataclysmic changes are on the horizon. Marketers may be facing shifts in consumer and communications patterns for which there are no precedents and for which they are ill prepared.[18]

## THAT TECTONIC SHIFT WAS THE INTERNET

Since the mid-1990s the internet has had tremendous impact on culture, commerce and marketing.

In 1985 America Online, Inc. began offering internet services.[19]

By 1994, more than 1,500 web servers were online and the Internet was referred to as the Information Superhighway.[20]

In 1997 there were a million websites[21], including the first blogs.[22] AOL Instant Messenger[23] let people chat and sixdegrees.com let users set up profiles and list friends.[24]

In 1998, Google Launched as a major search engine.[25]

In 2000, despite the dot.com bubble, 70 million computers were connected to the internet.[26]

In the February 26, 1995 issue of Newsweek, Clifford Stoll wrote in his article "Why the Web Won't Be Nirvana":

> After two decades online, I'm perplexed. It's not that I haven't had a gas of a good time on the Internet. I've met great people and even caught a hacker or two. But today, I'm uneasy about this most trendy and oversold community. Visionaries see a future of telecommuting workers, interactive libraries and multimedia classrooms. They speak of electronic town meetings and virtual communities. Commerce and business will shift from offices and malls to networks and modems. And the freedom of digital networks will make government more democratic.
>
> Baloney. Do our computer pundits lack all common sense? The truth is no online database will replace your daily newspaper, no CD-ROM can take the place of a competent teacher and no computer network will change the way government works.[27]

Clifford Stoll, it turns out, was wrong. By the turn of the Millennium the world and the future of marketing was forever changed and by 2015 the visionaries Stoll disbelieved were proven right.

The early 2000s saw the rise of social media—Friendster, MySpace, LinkedIn—culminating in the birth of Facebook in 2004 and its steady growth: 100 million in 2008, 845 million in 2011, and 1 billion in 2012 and 1.35 billion monthly by the 4th Quarter of 2014.[28]

In 1998 there were 2 million web sites, including Google which launched that year. By 2000 there were 17 million, almost 65 million in 2005, almost 207 million in 2010 and over 1.2 billion in March 2015.[29]

YouTube began in 2005. By 2015, it had over one billion monthly users and 300 hours of video were uploaded to YouTube every minute.[30]

Twitter began in 2007. By 2015 it had 288 million active users sending 500 milion tweets each day.[31]

In 2000 the estimated population of Internet users was 394 million. By 2015 it had reached over 2.9 billion.[32]

March 12, 2014 marked the 25th anniversary of the World Wide Web. According to the PewResearch Internet Project 87% of American Adults use the internet.

*In a new national survey to mark the 25th anniversary of the Web, Pew Research finds further confirmation of the incredible spread and impact of the internet:*

***Adoption:*** *87% of American adults now use the internet, with near-saturation usage among those living in households earning $75,000 or more (99%), young adults ages 18-29 (97%), and those with college degrees (97%). Fully 68% of adults connect to the internet with mobile devices like smartphones or tablet computers.*

*The adoption of related technologies has also been extraordinary: Over the course of Pew Research Center polling, adult ownership of cell phones has risen from 53% in our first survey in 2000 to 90% now. Ownership of smartphones has grown from 35% when we first asked in 2011 to 58% now.*

*Impact:* Asked for their overall judgment about the impact of the internet, toting up all the pluses and minuses of connected life, the public's verdict is overwhelmingly positive:

90% of internet users say the internet has been a good thing for them personally and only 6% say it has been a bad thing, while 3% volunteer that it has been some of both.

76% of internet users say the internet has been a good thing for society, while 15% say it has been a bad thing and 8% say it has been equally good and bad.[33]

As the internet has become more important in our lives, we have increasingly wanted the convenience of taking it with us. Today, massive volumes of content are shared in real time across digital platforms and social media. We live in a tech-savvy and social-media driven world. Consumers hold immense power to promote or devastate products, professionals and businesses.

Apple released the first iPhone in 2007[34] and the first iPad tablet computer with advanced multimedia and Internet capabilities in 2010.[35]

By the end of 2010, more people got their news from the Internet than from newspapers.[36]

By 2013 about half of Facebook and Twitter users got news on those sites.[37]

By 2014, according to the PewResearch Internet Project, of the 58% of Americans who had smart phones, 34% used their phone as their primary point of access to the internet over other devices such as laptop or desktop computers.[38]

In this environment it is crucial to understand your consumer's world, daily behaviors and motivations. Their needs and wants drive the way they connect, influence their behavior and communications. In this environment successful businesses listen more than they talk. They build relationships and offer content that has value to their target audience.

Your brand—self-knowledge, promise, consistency, authenticity and honest communication—provides needed stability in this rapidly changing environment.

We will talk more about the power and complications that the internet brings in Chapter 2.

## A LOOK AHEAD

We've established the importance of the concept of integrated branding as a method for presenting yourself and your business to prospective clients. The remaining chapters of this book will lead you through the steps necessary to develop your own brand.

**NOTES**

CHAPTER 2

# CLEARING THE CLUTTER
## Where Does Branding Begin?

## DEFINING "BRAND" TODAY

A brand is like a car: it has both fashion and function. It needs to have both the attractive appearance and the solid mechanics to satisfy the consumer. Like a car, a good brand suits your purpose in both form and function. You wouldn't expect a Tesla to serve as a farm truck any more than you would expect to drive a kids' carpool in a Miata. The same is true with brands.

### AN EFFECTIVE BRAND WORKS FOR YOU

A brand that works is based on who you are, what you do and why it matters that you do it. Your brand must connect and resonate with clients and keep them coming back because you offer them something that benefits them.

> *Success means never letting the competition define you. Instead you have to define yourself based on a point of view you care deeply about.*
> *– Tom Chappell, founder of Tom's of Maine*

Your brand is a combination of two things: 1) the promise you make to deliver a specific set of features, benefits and services to your clients and 2) what people experience with you—what they think, feel and perceive about you.

> *A brand for a company is like a reputation for a person. You earn reputation by trying to do hard things well.*
> *– Jeff Bezos, founder of Amazon*

When all the brand jargon is cleared away two key elements remain: Brand Strategy and Brand Communication. Brand Strategy is the plan that guides your work and informs your Brand Communication. Brand Communication allows you say the right thing—to the right people—in the right way—at the right time.

In this chapter we will look at why branding is worth the investment and what it means to have a brand work for you.

## STEP 1: BRAND STRATEGY

Your brand is more than your logo, name or tagline—it's the entire experience people have with you. Your brand lives in every day-to-day interaction you have with your target market, through:

- Your communication with clients and prospects
- The way your employees interact with customers
- Your client's opinion of you relative to your competition

Brand Strategy is simply the plan that guides how you will remain relevant and valuable to your clients and differentiated from others who offer similar services. It allows you to remain both consistent and flexible. It focuses on the long-term needs of your clients. It solves their problems rather than offering products.

Your brand strategy defines what you stand for, the promise you make and the personality you convey. Brand Strategy works from the inside out and is built on and incorporates your mission, vision, guiding principles, norms/culture, goals and values.

### BRAND STRATEGY GIVES YOU BOTH INTERNAL AND EXTERNAL BENEFITS

Brand Strategy is not just a marketing activity. It is an opportunity to build a strong, congruent business culture and a clear, vibrant personality within your target market. The prime objective of your brand strategy is to provide a compelling and unique customer experience that goes beyond the product or service itself. Defining your relationship with clients allows you to remain open to new ways of meeting their needs rather than being defined by your current products and services.

## BRAND STRATEGY GUIDES YOU

Your brand strategy gives you self-awareness about exactly who you are, what you do and who you want to work with. It gives you a framework for making decisions. It directs your actions. It helps you make good business choices across all aspects of your business.

Anyone who has sailed a small boat knows about tell-tails. They are the small bits of yarn or string attached as a pair on either side of the sail. When you are heading in the right direction and your sail is trimmed correctly the tell-tails flow straight back with the sail. If your sail is too far out, the tell-tail on the inside of the sail will flap. If the sail is too tight the outside tell-tail will flap. Watching your tell-tails lets you know when you have adjusted your sail correctly and are sailing most efficiently.

Your brand is like a tell-tail for your business. If you pay attention to your brand it will help you do the right thing.

## BRAND STRATEGY ALLOWS YOU TO CATCH THE ATTENTION OF THE RIGHT PEOPLE

At the most basic level your brand says who you are and what you do—but it does it in a way that makes you stand out from the crowd of others who do similar work. It gives you the right kind of visibility. It builds your reputation.

### Attractive and Distinctive

Your brand has two main jobs: to make you attractive and show that you are distinctive. You want to be similar enough to your target clients to be attractive to them and different enough from your competition to be distinctive.

FastCompany selected the "Top 100 Most Creative People in Business, 2014." Number 8 on the list was actress Anna Kendick (*Twilight, Up in the Air, Pitch Perfect, 1 & 2, Into the Woods*). Author Josh Eells writes of Kendrick:

> *If there's something about the concept of a personal brand that Kendrick still finds a little . . . uncool, she's also too smart to pretend it's not important. "I know the idea of a brand is something that I'm supposed to not care about," she says. "But I do think it's a part of my life, and I'm trying to just be in control of it, as opposed to ignoring it."*
>
> *Which prompts the question: What is the Anna Kendrick brand? In a nutshell, she's the girl who gets to do lots of glamorous stuff, but is supremely stoked about it. Her three most popular Instagram posts provide a nice case study: One is a photo of her scarfing down In-N-Out at Vanity Fair's Oscar party in March [2014], another is of her freaking*

*out while meeting Beyoncé at the Grammys, and the third is of a solid-gold macaroni pendant that Kraft sent her for being a vocal mac-and-cheese fan. What all three have in common: a (ahem) pitch-perfect mix of outsider awkwardness and insider cool. She's the girl at the party other girls wish they could be—and more important, the girl they think they could be.*[39]

### Like Me = Attractive

Social psychology has studied why we are attracted to some people and not to others. A model called *Similarity/Attraction Theory* explains that we are attracted to—and like—people who are similar to us. Anna Kendrick is attractive because she is *"the girl they think they could be."*

Many studies since the mid-1900s have confirmed this "birds of a feather flock together" theory. In general, people are most attracted to others who share similar attitudes to theirs.

There are several reasons for this:

- We feel less alone. "When we find that somebody else expresses the same attitudes and opinions we hold on an issue, we are given support for the notion that our own attitude is the correct one; the attitude is given social validation."[40]

- It's easier to predict future behavior in a person with similar attitudes—they are more knowable.

- People who share similar attitudes are more likely to be attracted to you—relationships are more likely to form and maintain over time.

We'll talk more about shared beliefs as a key element of attraction later in this chapter.

### We're not as rational as we'd like to believe

We are much less fact based and more emotional in our choices, attractions and the justification for how people act.

We tend to explain why we do what we do and why others do what they do by making assumptions and inferring the causes of those behaviors. This is human nature—*everyone* does it and we are rarely aware that we are doing it.

This phenomenon, called *Attribution Theory*, was first introduced by Austrian psychologist Fritz Heider (1896-1988) in his book *The Psychology of Interpersonal Relations* (1958) which explored the nature of interpersonal relationships and how we use "common sense" or "naïve psychology" to observe and explain behaviors. Fritz Heider's thinking influenced generations of psychologists who have further studied and defined attribution theory.

According to Heider we make assumptions about the causes of behaviors and people's motivation by assigning attributes to what they do. A nice way to think of this is that we are all amateur scientists, gathering and interpreting data from the world around us. It's important to note, however, that these interpretations are not related to facts. They are what we believe to be true.

Attributes can be internal (the person's ability, mood, personality, attitudes or disposition) or external (caused by a situation outside the person's control).

When we do poorly or make mistakes we tend to assume it is due to the circumstances of the situation. However when others do similar things we tend to assume it's because of who they are—or aren't.[41]

> For example: A mom is driving home from work on the freeway. Yesterday, she drove home tailgating and going too fast. She knew what she was doing but felt she had no choice. Her boss kept her late and she had to get to her children's daycare before it closed.

> Today she is irritated by a man driving a red sports car who is driving too fast and just cut her off. She thinks: "He is a thoughtless jerk."

This tendency to overestimate the internal and underestimate the external factors when explaining the behaviors of others is called the *Fundamental Attribution Error.* We assume the person in the red car is a jerk even though we know nothing about him and have no evidence that he is, in fact, a jerk.

Parents of teenagers frequently commit the Fundamental Attribution Error. It's easy to rant about your disrespectful, unthinking child who comes home late for curfew. However, if you ask the parents if they have ever been late their response will most likely be: "That's different."

They will go on to tell you the very good reason that was beyond their control. This is a second error—the *Self-Serving Bias* which says that we tend to equate our successes with internal factors and our failures with external situations. We see this in our speeding example. The mom thinks: "I'm not a bad person. I had to speed because of the circumstances I was in. It was really my boss' fault that I was speeding."  We don't consider that the man in the red sports car may have similar circumstances.[42]

**So what does this have to do with your brand?**

It shows the need for clarity and consistency. You don't want people to make assumptions about you. You want others to know who you are and what you offer. The more people understand about you the less likely they will be to attribute your behaviors improperly.

The best way to be clear and understandable is by making a brand promise that everyone understands.

---

**BRAND STRATEGY PROMPTS ACTION**

Your brand defines the response you want from customers and prospects. It offers a path for engagement and encourages participation.

You have an opportunity to prompt action through your brand but only if the desired actions and their benefits are clear and consistent. To stand out your brand has to:

- Get people's attention
- Convince them you have something important to offer them
- Make them remember you
- Convince them that you are the right choice for them

In their book, *Made To Stick: Why Some Ideas Survive and Others Die*, brothers Chip Heath and Dan Heath tell us:

*For an idea to stick, for it to be useful and lasting, it's got to make the audience:*

1. *Pay attention*
2. *Understand and remember it*
3. *Agree/Believe*
4. *Care*
5. *Be able to act on it* [43]

Their "Six Principles of Sticky Ideas" apply to brands as well as ideas:

1. Simplicity: stripping an idea down to its core so that it is easy for you to share and people to remember
2. Unexpected: surprising people, getting their attention and making them curious to learn more
3. Concreteness: concrete images based on the human senses help people understand and remember
4. Credibility: lets people agree and helps them believe
5. Emotions: people care because they feel something personal
6. Stories: connect, inspire, remind and inspire action[44]

---

While each of these points is significant, the stickiness of emotional connection is especially complicated and thought-provoking because people choose with their emotions more often than through facts and data.

Two researchers at the University of Texas—McCombs marketing professor Raj Raghunathan and Ph.D. student Szu-Chi Huang—addressed the issue of whether consumers make choices based on logic or emotion.

> *The fundamental question is whether consumers make their choices based on logical comparisons of performance, or are they emotional creatures who gravitate to products that appeal to their senses, feelings or moods? [Our]...research study...shows comparative features are important, but mostly as justification after a buyer makes a decision based on emotional response.*
>
> *"This is called post-hoc rationalization," said Raghunathan, "and it is found in every aspect of our life, whenever we made decisions. We are ruled by our emotions first, and then we build justifications for our response. You can see this happening in hiring decisions, dating, you name it."*
>
> *"In our society it is generally not considered justifiable to make a decision purely on an emotional response," he said. "We want to be considered scientific and rational, so we come up with reasons after the fact to justify our choice.*
>
> *"This process seems to be happening somewhat unconsciously, people are not really aware they're coming up with these justifications. What is even more interesting is that people who claim that emotions are not that important, who consider themselves to be really rational, are actually more prone to fall into this trap."*
>
> *Raghunathan and Huang believe this is because once someone has denied the possibility of making a decision based on emotion, there is no other option but to come up with justifications. "You paint yourself into a corner," he claims. "You want to portray yourself as this rational decision maker, but in reality, you're the one who's most likely to show post-hoc rationalization.*[45]

## BRAND STRATEGY MAKES A PROMISE

The heart and soul of your brand strategy is the promise you make to current and potential clients. Your brand says: "This is the promise I make and will fulfill." It tells people what you will do and what they will get. It tells them what their experience with you will be. To work it must convey a compelling benefit, be authentic and credible.

Developing an emotional brand attachment is a key factor for connecting with clients. Although the emotional decision to choose you and your brand comes first, it's human nature to look for facts to justify the decision. This is why clearly defining your brand promise is so important.

The promise you make must be aligned with the person you are trying to reach (*Similarity /Attraction Theory*). To be effective it must speak to the need of the person, business or group. A well-defined promise shows prospective clients why you are the right choice for them.

> ***Your premium brand had better be delivering something special, or it's not going to get the business. – Warren Buffett***

Apple, Volvo and Google have clear brand promises that are understandable to their customers and prospects.

- Apple promises the coolest, cutting edge computers and devices.
- Volvo promises that you and your family will be safe.
- Google promises to search the world's information to help you find exactly what you're looking for.

**Achieving Your Brand Promise Satisfies Your Clients**

Of course, you must follow through. The most important part of your brand promise is not making the promise, but keeping the promise. You can make the promise with words but you must keep your promise through action.  A broken promise is the kiss of death.

Nothing travels faster than the news that you promised one thing and delivered another—or didn't deliver at all.

In contrast, when customers' experiences match what they expect, you fulfill your promise. You have completed the circle of customer satisfaction. Because you have stated your brand promise clearly and then fulfilled it consistently your clients aren't making assumptions about what you do. Their attribution is borne out in fact.

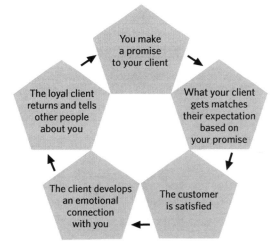

# Fulfilling Your Brand Promise = Good Business

## BP—a Promise Broken

*In 2000, BP (formerly British Petroleum) repositioned itself as an environmentally friendly energy company with the slogan "Beyond Petroleum." They rolled out this new promise in a $200 million marketing campaign that included a bright yellow and green icon. A major advertising campaign placed this new brand promise in front of consumers across all media channels.[46]*

*Two significant incidents showed BP's actions to be out of line with their promise of commitment to the environment and cleaner energy.*

*An explosion in April 2010 on BP's Deepwater Horizon offshore oil platform in the Gulf of Mexico caused the largest marine oil spill in history. The public response to the 2010 Gulf Oil spill was swift, definitive and harsh. The value of their stock dropped 50% in the seven weeks following the oil spill.[47]*

*Their brand was further tarnished when their involvement in the Alberta Oil Sands project came to light. This project attracted considerable controversy because of concerns about the impact on the environment and local communities.*

*In April 2014 BP quietly announced it was divesting its wind power assets. This followed their 2011 exit from solar power after 40 years.[48]*

## Velvet—a Promise Kept

*Velvet toilet paper (a U.K. brand) made a commitment to the environment that had a positive outcome in both audience perception and conversion to sales. The company used their desire to protect the environment as a way to become more distinctive and to attract customers who shared their values and the way they put those values into action.*

*They adopted the tag line "Luxury for you. Trees for the planet." to put their promise front and center. Their website (www.velvet-tissue.com/about) describes their environmental promise and how they are fulfilling it:*

*"You may have seen in our TV ads or on our website our 'three for one' promise of planting three trees for each one used; but what does that really mean? It means we have surpassed the standard industry practice of other industry tissue manufacturers, and since 2009 we have planted more than three million extra trees. Importantly, this commitment is not just about the past and present, but also the future."[49]*

*The public responded extremely well and the company reports its sales and market share increased.*

Loyal clients are the backbone of your company. They bring repeat business and make referrals to others. They understand, appreciate and advocate for your brand.

Through your brand you create a consciousness, an image, and an awareness of your business in the mind of your loyal clients. But this is not a one-time thing. It is important to build client loyalty in every client interaction, build your relationship with your best clients and increase your value in their minds.

### Client Satisfaction vs. Client Loyalty

Before we delve further into client loyalty we need to look at the difference between client satisfaction and client loyalty (and you want both).

Client loyalty is a behavior—repeatedly buying from the same source. Client satisfaction is an attitude based on the person's experience as a client. Satisfied clients are happy, content, pleased, fulfilled by their experience. This is directly related to the congruence they feel between what they expect (your promise) and what they receive (delivery on your promise).

Unfortunately, client satisfaction doesn't always result in client loyalty. Customers' buying behavior may be related to other factors.

Satisfied customers may not be loyal. Their customer experience with a business may meet or exceed their expectations but they purchase from that business only sporadically.

Similarly, a loyal customer isn't necessarily satisfied. They may have specific products or services that do not meet their expectations yet these are outweighed by other factors, such as convenience or price, that drive them to continue to repeat their business.

---

### Where Do You Buy Your Coffee?

*Coffee buying behavior is a good example of loyal vs. satisfied. If you ask, most people will tell you they have a favorite coffee shop. They can—and will—tell you all the things about the coffee, the service and the environment that they like. If you ask them if they always go there for coffee they say: "No." Asked why, they may tell you a variety of reasons, ranging from convenience: "I'd have to drive too far out of my way on my way to work." to price: "I only splurge on weekends."*

---

**Building Loyalty**

As we have seen, emotions play a large part in decision-making. Laurie Young writes in her article, "How to Foster Brand Loyalty Effectively":

> *Customers need something to be loyal to; something with which they can create an emotional bond. That something is brand. There is evidence that people can become loyal to product, corporate, service and consumer brands. In this context, that means choosing the use of one brand above others, sometimes with little explicit thought about how or why. This is often an unconscious emotional choice by the customer, which is enormously profitable for the supplier.*[50]

A key factor in brand loyalty is the congruence in perceived values between your target audience and you. Howard Schultz, in his book Pour *Your Heart Into It: How Starbucks Built a Company One Cup at a Time*, writes: "Mass advertising can help build brands, but authenticity is what makes them last. If people believe they share values with a company, they will stay loyal to the brand."[51]

In a study of over 7,000 consumers, researchers Karen Freeman, Patrick Spenner and Anna Bird found that companies often have the wrong ideas about how best to engage with their customers. Writing about their research findings in the *Harvard Business Review* (May 23, 2012) they discussed the myth that frequent interactions build relationships. Instead they found that shared values build relationships.

> *A shared value is a belief that both the brand and consumer have about a brand's higher purpose or broad philosophy. For example, Pedigree Dog Food's shared value is a belief that every dog deserves a loving home. Southwest Airlines' shared value revolves around the democratization of air travel.*

> *Of the consumers in our study who said they have a brand relationship, 64% cited shared values as the primary reason. That's far and away the largest driver. Meanwhile, only 13% cited frequent interactions with the brand as a reason for having a relationship.*[52]

One of the best ways to build loyalty is to be consistent—in your quality, your responsiveness and the delivery of your goods or services.

- By doing this you are staying true to your brand and fulfilling the promise you make through everything you do and say.

- This keeps your clients happy and builds a foundation for a lasting, meaningful, productive relationship with them.

- It keeps them coming back and makes you the one they recommend to their friends.

Another way to build loyalty is to showcase your value. Make sure your best clients understand how you make their business more successful and their life easier. This does not need to be flashy or overt.

- Become a solution rather than an expense by showing what not using your product or service costs their business.

- Position yourself as a partner in reaching their business goals.

- Show them how investing in you comes back to them in increased profitability, decreased stress and long-term sustainability.

Congruence, shared values and relationship, based on a strong brand promise that is fulfilled in every interaction, makes you the one clients remain loyal to and recommend to their friends and colleagues.

## STEP 2: BRAND COMMUNICATION

A brand that communicates well says the right things to the right people at the right time in the right place.

Every business and professional has a brand whether they manage it or not. A brand isn't a made-up thing. A brand encapsulates your purpose, actions, values and personality. If you don't understand and communicate your brand effectively you risk having some-one do it for you and they may not get it right. Anyone who has read a bad online review knows the power of one bad customer experience.

This misalignment of purpose and experience comes from two critical missteps:

1) Not understanding yourself (what you offer and what you do differently from others).

   Understanding yourself—knowing what makes you attractive and what makes you distinctive—is essential before you can communicate these to your market. As we saw in Chapter 1 you need to be more than just excellent or the cheapest or willing to be what a prospective client might want. In order to succeed you need to be yourself.

2) Not communicating who you are to the people you want as your customers.

   It's not enough to know who you are. You need to communicate who you are to others. They must understand your purpose and your promise and they must be convinced that you will deliver on that promise.

Alastair Herbert and Ali Goode, of Linguabrand, study brand language. In their article, "Brand Communication: Mind Your Brand Language," they discuss how often generic language is used to describe what brands do and the problems that result.

> *What is your brand talking about? It's a remarkably obvious question, but, too often, most can only guess. The result is brands clustering around generic ideas. That explains why most brand language is so repetitive, even approaching being boring. Our analysis has put over four million brand words through software to measure brand agendas. On average, they're 54% generic. That's the same as saying 46% distinctive. So, right now, brands are investing more in saying the same as competitors than they are trying to say something unique.*

> *So how do you find concepts, ideas and topics that are distinctive? Difference and similarity are two sides of the same coin. Brand difference is measured by first identifying the market generic agenda. This is a virtual least-competitive position, made up of concepts too widespread to be owned. It's really useful for pointing you in the direction of distinctiveness. Of course, there will be some 'must-have' generics. But these should only account for up to 34% of any agenda. That's a reduction of 20 percentage points from 54%. This is the brand agenda gap.[53]*

Communication is more than the words used. It's also the style and tone of voice. Few people think about this extremely important aspect of communication. Each of us, as an individual, has a distinctive voice. A well-developed brand voice cues people to your distinctiveness and indicates what you stand for—your values, beliefs and promise. Herbert and Goode describe this phenomenon:

> *The way brands talk about their agenda is their tone of voice – the style it's delivered in. And that's why it's so closely associated with brand values. If your bank talks to you in the style of an old friend, it's immediately irksome but, for the most part, tone of voice is received subliminally. Having a tone of voice is unavoidable – every brand has, even if it's inconsistent or inappropriate.*

> *Most conversations about tone of voice revolve around opinions. People use terms like 'confident' or 'approachable'. But what do these ideas mean? What's the difference between an 'approachable' brand and 'friendly' brand, for instance? Another bad habit is comparing your brand's tone with others. Apple, Virgin and Innocent are quoted frequently, but this is largely unhelpful. You can never be another brand; but you can find and define yourself. And that starts with understanding where you fit in right now. As with all brand language, this means understanding the competitive context.*

*The power companies spend more on language than most. And as a sector, it has worked – they sound good against other markets. But, listen more closely and you find all the brands have the same tone of voice. So, despite the investment, they've turned brand language into bland language.*

*At its best, tone of voice delivers language reinforcing your brand values. Values are often a set of aspirations, often at odds with how your brand is actually talking...When tone of voice echoes your values, your verbal identity is really coming together.*[54]

## COMMUNICATING YOUR BRAND PURPOSE

It is important that your communication tells authentic stories about who you are. The worst thing you can do is fabricate. Consumers can see through the "spin" and will reject what they see as inauthentic. What you communicate needs to be real and true.

A first step is to define your purpose, first for yourself and then in your communication. What do you want others to know about you? How will you communicate your distinctiveness, including what you offer on both a functional and an emotional level?

The next step is to identify key information about your target audience:

- What do they need and want?
- What do they care about?
- What are their values?

What is the intersection between your unique offering and what your target audience needs and wants? Identifying this intersection helps you define your brand purpose.

A brand's purpose is to make positive impacts for their clients whether it is for one person, a company, an industry or the world. It is up to you to define the magnitude of your brand's purpose but no matter how big that purpose is, it is up to you to deliver on it. It is part of your brand promise.

Your Unique Offering

Customer Needs and Wants

Brand Purpose

The following examples show how companies understand their purpose and what that purpose means to their clients and prospective clients:

- We want our company to be the first name customers think of when they start a new home improvement project.

- We want people to connect to our product in an elemental and emotional way because of its intrinsic character and beauty.

- We watch trends and innovations in our industry so that we can be the first to offer them to our clients.

- We want to be our client's organizational development strategist and their trusted advisor.

- We want to offer easy solutions for clients that also reduce waste, minimize chemicals, and conserve water and other natural resources.

Brand purpose integrated into all communication brings your brand promise to life for your target audience and stakeholder groups and increases the connection between you and your best clients and target audience.

## HOW THE INTERNET HAS CHANGED BRAND COMMUNICATION

These concepts hold true no matter how you interact or where you communicate. They are especially true in online communication and social media where the focus is not on stating what you have to offer but in staying in the conversation in a meaningful, attractive and distinctive way. These online communications channels are growing more powerful and important every month.

Branding changed in the mid-20th century from defining differences in quality to selling an image. In the same way the internet has changed relationships and communication. Companies traditionally told you who they were and what to think about them. The internet provides a path for discovering what a company offers and how it is similar or different from others.

As we saw in Chapter 1 the internet has changed the relationship consumers have with brands. Traditional marketing channels including TV, radio and print advertising, direct mailing and printed promotional materials have given way to consumer initiated interactions on the internet. This includes searchable websites, social media and business review sites.

Whether you are looking for a doctor, a hotel in Alaska or a dog breeder, the internet can educate you, connect you and offer reviews and opinions from other consumers. This means solid brand strategy has to be in place and brand promise and fulfillment of that promise is even more important.

## People educate themselves online about products and services

They research, follow blogs, compare, read reviews and listen to what others have to say. Retailers, including Verizon and Best Buy, let you evaluate options and compare features when shopping online. By the time consumers make first contact, they are ready to buy or have very specific questions they want answered.

Olympic Hot Tub Company, started in Seattle in 1977, is the oldest spa and hot tub company in the Northwest. Their tagline "Relax for Life®" extends from their showrooms (where they offer the opportunity for people to "test soak" before they buy) to their website where customers can learn about products, health benefits and much more.

Their website is the entry point for many of their customers who arrive at their store with knowledge of options, information on how products compare to those sold by other retailers and specific questions.

Their blog educates while engaging prospects and maintaining relationships with customers. It covers a variety of topics including hot tub care, connecting with your teen in the hot tub and the role of hot tubs in reducing sleep problems.

Co-owner Alice Cunningham who writes the blog sees a direct correlation between the blog's popularity and high SEO (search engine optimization) and sales. "We dominate the search for 'hot tub.' Our web traffic is really high and we dominate page one for many searches."[55]

**In the past companies initiated communication with the consumer.** Companies decided how to connect with consumers through market research and made those connections through advertising. Now consumers use search engines to find and initiate contact with products and companies. They reach out because they are curious and they use online resources to find answers.

*. . . a recent Corporate Executive Board study of more than 1,400 B2B customers found that those customers completed, on average, nearly 60% of a typical purchasing decision —researching solutions, ranking options, setting requirements, benchmarking pricing, and so on— before even having a conversation with a supplier.*[56]

Most of us have had the experience of following a link and ending up in an unexpected place. We search for a specific thing but along the way we "run into" something that catches our attention and that leads to another interesting thing. The down-side for us is lost time but the up-side for the sites we land on is increased visibility and possibly a new fan.

Darla Luke writes about this experience on her blog *See Jane Publish*:

> *Have you ever done this? In doing research for what propels self-published authors and/ or books to the USA Today Top 150 list, I opened up my internet search engine and typed in Jennifer Ashley ... wallah, in 3.8 seconds I'm presented with 100 links to Jennifer. Since I'm researching, I clicked on the link to Jennifer Ashley, Romance Writer. An hour and many clicks later, I've read her blog back to 2010 and am now reading an excerpt of one of her books on her website. (BTW, she hasn't blogged in a long time, probably too busy writing fantastic books!)*
>
> *The next thing I know, more than two hours have gone by without me knowing about it! Oh, not to mention all the money I've spent because I love books! And that research I started? Not quite finished yet. Too much information (and books to read ... did I mention how much I love books?)*[57]

It's not enough to talk—you have to listen. Social media has changed market research. Participants self-select. Consumers share what they like and dislike and what offerings they would like to see from companies. If companies aren't listening they are missing key information. Social media offers an opportunity to have conversations with the end user rather than broadcast what they want consumers to know. Not taking this opportunity is an opportunity missed.

Taco Bell listens and communicates using Twitter, Instagram, YouTube, Tumblr and Facebook. They are known for their quirky humor and engaging style. Nick Tran leads a small social media team for the company. Tran's LinkedIn profile describes him as the Social Media Lead for Taco Bell Corp. responsible for Strategy, Community Management, and Future Social Business Team.

What this means is that he and his team have developed a personality for Taco Bell on social media. That personality is fun, witty, quirky and somewhat tongue-in-cheek.

Sam Laird, *Mashable.com*, reports that "Taco Bell has gained a well-earned reputation for being one of the wittiest, sassiest brands on social media. The company is always quick with some humorous banter for followers—or pretty much anyone else who tweets about tacos."[58]

The team's goal is to engage, not just "tell." With over 10 million Likes on Facebook and 1.2 million followers on Twitter it appears to be working.

A fan's post on Taco Bell's Facebook page is an extreme example of connection with a brand:

> Marco: I love you Taco Bell. So much.
>
> Taco Bell: How much, Marco?
>
> Marco: So much that you're tattooed on my body FOREVER.[59]

Few companies will have customers who express their love through tattoos. Many can develop strong, lasting relationships through their brand communication on social media.

## DEVELOPING YOUR OWN BRAND

The goal of this book is to give you a structure for developing your brand strategy and brand communication. The following chapters will guide you through a series of exercises that provide a template for doing this.

## NOTES

## CHAPTER 3

# STAND OUT FROM THE CROWD
## Creating an Identity That Works for You

Your brand tells people who you are and what you do in a way that makes you stand out from the crowd. It gives you the right kind of visibility and builds your reputation. For your brand to work for you, it must define who you are and what sets you apart.

This chapter will guide you through the process of building a brand strategy using your curiosity, knowledge, creativity and patience.

## THE BRANDING PROCESS

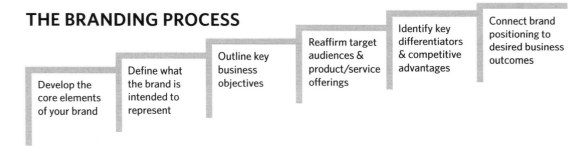

Develop the core elements of your brand → Define what the brand is intended to represent → Outline key business objectives → Reaffirm target audiences & product/service offerings → Identify key differentiators & competitive advantages → Connect brand positioning to desired business outcomes

## WHO YOU ARE

To define your brand you need to assess who you are, what makes you attractive and what makes you distinctive. The exercises in this chapter can help you unearth your brand.

### VALUES

Knowing what you believe in is the first step in understanding who you are. Writing a values statement requires you to define your core philosophy and beliefs.

**Google's Values**

1. *Focus on the user and all else will follow.*
2. *It's best to do one thing really, really well.*
3. *Fast is better than slow.*
4. *Democracy on the web works.*
5. *You don't need to be at your desk to need an answer.*
6. *You can make money without doing evil.*
7. *There's always more information out there.*
8. *The need for information crosses all borders.*
9. *You can be serious without a suit.*
10. *Great just isn't good enough.*[60]

**Whole Foods' Values**

1. *We Sell the Highest Quality Natural and Organic Products Available.*

2. *We Satisfy, Delight and Nourish Our Customers.*

3. *We Support Team Member Happiness and Excellence.*

4. *We Create Wealth Through Profits & Growth.*

5. *We Serve and Support Our Local and Global Communities.*

6. *We Practice and Advance Environmental Stewardship.*

7. *We Create Ongoing Win-Win Partnerships with Our Suppliers.*

8. *We Promote the Health of Our Stakeholders Through Healthy Eating Education.*[61]

Brainstorm a list of your values

Select your core values

_____

_____

_____

_____

Combine them into a values statement

_____

_____

_____

_____

## NORMS

Norms can best be described as 'the way you do things.' Norms are your customs and traditions expressed through your behavior; your values in action. They are reflected in your conduct, ways of communicating, the way you dress and your preferred surroundings.

In groups, including companies, norms are informal guidelines about what is considered normal social behavior and form the basis of collective expectations the members of the group. Over time, groups develop ways of interacting with each other that become habits and eventually behavioral expectations. They, in effect, exert social pressure on the individual to conform.

Casual Friday in a company or monthly potlucks enhance camaraderie. Behavior in meetings, the level of formality between supervisors and staff and the degree of independent decision making are all examples of a company's norms.

For individuals, norms are more about personal preferences. They are both reflected by and influence daily routines. Norms are what make a person comfortable and productive.

For both individuals and groups, norms are seen in a variety of behaviors:

- Daily routine
- Decision making
- Project management
- Work habits

- Appearance
- Performance
- Interpersonal relationships
- Conflict resolution

A night owl may write or finish paperwork in the middle of the night when things are quiet and interruptions are few. An early bird may hop out of bed and go straight to the gym because that is the person's highest energy time of day.

The first step is to understand your personal norms and observe the similarities and differences between your norms and those of groups (work, social and family) you are part of. This entails a state of awareness of what is happening around you without judgment or attachment.

The ability to observe the norms of individuals or groups will enable you to see a larger context of the work being done and see expanded possibilities for action, whether with clients, in work groups or as part of a company. Without this ability we tend to reflexively defend our norms as truths rather than a set of behaviors that have evolved over time to give us agility, accountability and functionality.

## DEFINE YOUR NORMS

Make a list of your personal norms—the ways you prefer to 'do things.'

_____

_____

_____

_____

_____

_____

_____

Next, put your norms into groups and title each group:

Group 1:

1. _____

2. _____

3. _____

4. _____

5. _____

6. _____

Group 2:

1. _____

2. _____

3. _____

4. _____

5. _____

6. _____

## Group 3:

1. _____
2. _____
3. _____
4. _____
5. _____
6. _____

## Group 4:

1. _____
2. _____
3. _____
4. _____
5. _____
6. _____

## Group 5:

1. _____
2. _____
3. _____
4. _____
5. _____
6. _____

Group 6:

1. _____
2. _____
3. _____
4. _____
5. _____
6. _____

## Vision and Mission

At some point we have all gone through the exercise of defining vision and mission statements. Maybe you have helped write one for a business or a charity organization.

Your vision and mission are the start of any business plan. They direct your actions, keep you focused and help you stay consistent. They act as a filter for all your communications about who you are. They are often posted on websites for clients and prospects.

### YOUR VISION STATEMENT PROVIDES DIRECTION FOR YOUR FUTURE

A vision statement defines a point you want to reach. It is aspirational. It reflects your interest, passion and direction. It provides guidance and inspiration to look ahead and to the future. A vision statement:

- Gives shape and direction to your future
- Defines what do you want to become
- Describes the world as you would like it to be
- Stretches your capabilities and image—it's the challenge you give yourself

### Vision Example: Microsoft

*Our vision is to create innovative technology that is accessible to everyone and that adapts to each person's needs. Accessible technology eliminates barriers for people with disabilities and it enables individuals to take full advantage of their capabilities.*[62]

**– Bill Gates, Chairman**

## WRITE YOUR VISION STATEMENT.

*(If you already have a vision statement, copy it below.)*

Keep these things in mind:

- Dream big
- Think about where you want to be in the future (3, 5, or 10 years)
- Infuse your statement with the passion and excitement you feel
- Focus on success

## MISSION STATEMENT: DEFINES WHAT YOU DO

A mission statement is a key tool that captures—in a few concise sentences—your fundamental business goals and the philosophies that underlying them. It defines what your business is all about to your clients, employees, stakeholders and the community. Your mission statement:

- Expresses your philosophy and purpose
- Brings your goals into focus and your values into action
- Describes how you do it and with whom
- Defines why are you different, unique

### Mission Example: Microsoft

*At Microsoft, our mission is to enable people and businesses throughout the world to realize their full potential. We consider our mission statement a commitment to our customers. We deliver on that commitment by striving to create technology that is accessible to everyone—of all ages and abilities. Microsoft is one of the industry leaders in accessibility innovation and in building products that are safer and easier to use.*[64]

### Mission Example: Starbucks

*Our mission: to inspire and nurture the human spirit – one person, one cup and one neighborhood at a time.*[65]

### WRITE YOUR MISSION STATEMENT.
*(If you already have a mission statement, copy on the following page.)*

Keep these things in mind:

- Your values
- What inspires you
- Be specific about what you do and the value you bring clients
- Be clear and concise

_____

_____

_____

_____

_____

_____

_____

_____

_____

_____

_____

## GUIDING PRINCIPLES: DEEPLY HELD, DRIVING FORCES

Guiding principles give you direction—a moral compass even—no matter what changes occur in goals, strategies, work methods or other parts of your business. They are the foundation for your business.

- Reflect your values and norms
- Provide a structure for the work you do
- Are action oriented

---

### Example: Microsoft

- *Human Rights*
- *Responsible Sourcing*
- *Environmental Sustainability*

- *Integrity & Governance*
- *Political Engagement*
- *Our People*[66]

---

**Example: Starbucks**

(Starbucks publishes their guiding principles on their website and posts them in their stores.)

*Here are the principles of how we live that every day:*

*Our Coffee: It has always been, and will always be, about quality. We're passionate about ethically sourcing the finest coffee beans, roasting them with great care, and improving the lives of people who grow them. We care deeply about all of this; our work is never done.*

*Our Partners: We're called partners, because it's not just a job, it's our passion. Together, we embrace diversity to create a place where each of us can be ourselves. We always treat each other with respect and dignity. And we hold each other to that standard.*

*Our Customers: When we are fully engaged, we connect with, laugh with, and uplift the lives of our customers – even if just for a few moments. Sure, it starts with the promise of a perfectly made beverage, but our work goes far beyond that. It's really about human connection.*

*Our Stores: When our customers feel this sense of belonging, our stores become a haven, a break from the worries outside, a place where you can meet with friends. It's about enjoyment at the speed of life – sometimes slow and savored, sometimes faster. Always full of humanity.*

*Our Neighborhood: Every store is part of a community, and we take our responsibility to be good neighbors seriously. We want to be invited in wherever we do business. We can be a force for positive action – bringing together our partners, customers, and the community to contribute every day. Now we see that our responsibility – and our potential for good – is even larger. The world is looking to Starbucks to set the new standard, yet again. We will lead.*

*Our Shareholders: We know that as we deliver in each of these areas, we enjoy the kind of success that rewards our shareholders. We are fully accountable to get each of these elements right so that Starbucks – and everyone it touches – can endure and thrive.*[67]

**What are your guiding principles?**

Using your mission, vision, values and norms as a guide, develop three to five guiding principles that will motivate you to action. Try to keep them short, understandable and measurable.

1. _____

2. _____

3. _____

4. _____

5. _____

## WHAT SETS YOU APART

### BRAND ASSETS

Your brand is more than your expertise and competence. It encompasses a set of Brand Assets that define how you are different from others who have the similar skills.

Brand Assets define others' experiences with you. They are intangibles that are unique to you and provide the "value added" component to working with you.

Brand Assets can be divided into 4 categories:

1. What makes you **Unique**

2. Why you are **Believable** to others

3. What makes you **Memorable**

4. Why you are **Important**

While it is vital to understand the features and benefits of what you offer, these are only a piece of the customer's decision-making process. Emotional responses are at least as important. (See page 25 for more on emotional decision-making) Brand assets are emotional connectors and an essential part of how customers make decisions.

As you complete the following exercise, think of the brand assets of the three real estate agents discussed on page 7—the Neighborhood Specialist, the Market Expert and the Supporter. What assets enhance the expertise and experience of each?

**YOUR BRAND ASSETS**

Write down what makes you:

UNIQUE

_____

_____

_____

_____

_____

_____

MEMORABLE

_____

_____

_____

_____

_____

_____

BELIEVABLE

_____

_____

_____

_____

_____

_____

IMPORTANT

_____

_____

_____

_____

_____

_____

## PERSONALITY

Your personality is the set of characteristics others see in you. It's the face you show the outside world that reflects your norms and values. Individuals, companies, services, products and organizations all have their own distinct personalities that fall into three categories:

Internal—your own thoughts, feelings and beliefs

External—how you want the world to see you

Attributed—how others see you

The personality of your brand is most effective if all three of these are in alignment.

Researchers since the 1880s have tried to determine whether there is a set of personality traits that can be objectively determined. In the 1960s, Ernest Tupes and Raymond Christal, using a personality test develop in 1940 by Raymond Cattell called the *Sixteen Personality Factor Questionnaire*[68] found five recurring factors generally referred to as the Big Five Personality Traits[69]:

- Extroversion (also called Surgery): traits include assertive, talkative, energetic, sociable

- Agreeableness: traits include agreeable, compassionate, cooperative

- Conscientiousness: traits include efficient, thorough, planful, organized

- Emotional Stability: refers to the degree of emotional stability and impulse control

- Openness to Experience: traits include imaginative, intellectual curiosity, creativity

In a 1997 study, Jennifer Aaker defined a corresponding framework for brand personality, which she defined as "the set of human characteristics associated with a brand."

Sincerity—down-to-earth, honest, wholesome and cheerful

Excitement—daring, spirited, imaginative, up-to-date

Competence—reliable, intelligent, successful

Sophistication—upper-class, charming

Ruggedness—outdoorsy[70]

## PERSONALITY QUIZ

Check all of the personality traits that you think apply to you.

- ❏ **Honesty:** Having integrity and keeping one's promise.
- ❏ **Courtesy:** Being thoughtful of others.
- ❏ **Responsibility:** Being accountable for duties and following through with your duties.
- ❏ **Compatibility:** Being in harmony with others and having the ability to work well with others.
- ❏ **Loyalty:** Showing devotion to people and/or things.
- ❏ **Enthusiasm:** Having a strong affinity towards and eagerness/willingness to work with others or things.
- ❏ **Open-mindedness:** Being receptive and interested in the opinions and ideas of others.
- ❏ **Self-Control:** Controlling your own actions and feelings.
- ❏ **Influence:** Motivating or encouraging others.
- ❏ **Initiative:** Starting thoughts and/or actions.
- ❏ **Adaptability:** Making changes when necessary.
- ❏ **Industriousness:** Being consistently active and getting work done.
- ❏ **Carefulness:** Giving watchful attention to people and/or things and doing things properly.
- ❏ **Self-Reliance:** Having trust in one's self to do things independently and feel confident about them.
- ❏ **Compassion:** Having sympathy and feelings for people with problems.
- ❏ **Dedication:** Being seriously devoted to causes and/or goals.
- ❏ **Competitiveness:** Striving to win.
- ❏ **Patience:** Being able to wait and taking time to do things.
- ❏ **Perfectionism:** Trying to achieve the highest possible degree of excellence.
- ❏ **Courage:** Meeting danger or difficulties in spite of fear.
- ❏ **Decisiveness:** Making decisions promptly and definitely.
- ❏ **Drive:** Having the energy to get things done.
- ❏ **Perseverance:** Being persistent in pursuit of tasks.
- ❏ **Physical Challenge:** Enjoys physical challenges.
- ❏ **Calmness:** Being serene.

**PERSONALITY QUIZ** *continued*

❏ **Stability:** Being constant in responses.

❏ **Help Society:** Doing something to contribute to the betterment of the world.

❏ **Help Others:** being involved in helping other people in a direct way, either individually or in small groups.

❏ **Public Contact:** Have a lot of day-to-day contact with people.

❏ **Work with Others:** Having close working relationships with a group, work as a team toward common goals.

❏ **Affiliation:** Being recognized as a member of a particular organization.

❏ **Friendships:** Developing close personal relationships with people.

❏ **Competition:** Engaging in activities that pit abilities against others where there are clear win-and-lose outcomes.

❏ **Make Decisions:** Having the power to decide courses of action, policies, etc.

❏ **Work under Pressure:** Working in situations where time pressure is prevalent and/or the quality of work is judged critically.

❏ **Influence People:** Being in a position to change attitudes or opinions of other people.

❏ **Work Alone:** Doing projects independently, without any significant amount of contact with others.

❏ **Knowledge:** Engaging in the pursuit of knowledge, truth and understanding.

❏ **Artistic Creativity:** Engaging in creative work in any of several art forms.

❏ **Aesthetics:** Noticing the beauty of things, ideas, etc.

❏ **Stability:** Preferring a routine that is largely predictable and not likely to change over a long period of time.

❏ **Recognition:** Being recognized in some visible or public way.

❏ **Excitement:** Experiencing a high degree of (or frequent) exhilaration.

❏ **Adventure:** Enjoying frequent risk-taking.

❏ **Profit, Gain:** Interested in accumulating money or other material gain.

❏ **Independence:** Being able to determine the nature of work without significant direction from others; not having to do what others say.

❏ **Moral Fulfillment:** Wanting to contribute significantly to a set of moral standards.

Select your top 3 personality traits: Choose the top three to five (you can combine two or three if you see them as connected).

1. _____

2. _____

3. _____

How are these traits important to your brand?

_____

_____

_____

_____

What actionable things would showcase your personality?

_____

_____

_____

_____

How do your final traits relate to the Big Five Personality Traits and/or Aaker's Brand Personality Framework?

_____

_____

_____

_____

_____

Next, talk to people who know you/your business well. How do they describe you? Does their reflection match your description of your personality?

_____

_____

_____

How do these things that you have discovered about yourself inform the process of defining your brand strategy? We will see in subsequent chapters.

**NOTES**

_____

_____

_____

_____

_____

_____

_____

_____

_____

_____

_____

_____

_____

_____

_____

CHAPTER 4

# THE CLIMATE THAT SURROUNDS YOU
## Understanding the Context for Your Brand

## KNOW YOUR MARKET

In Chapter 3 you worked on the ancient Greek concept "Know Thyself." But it is not enough to pay attention to the internal. It is also important to look beyond yourself. In this chapter you will turn your focus outward to understand your market and the place your business fits in that market.

By going through this process you will have a better understanding of how best to choose your clients and fulfill your promise to them.

### INTERNAL AND EXTERNAL MARKET CLIMATE

You can enhance your success by understanding and adapting to the external drivers/ inhibitors of growth. These include:

- The changing demands and needs of consumers
- The emergence of new market conditions (These can include economic conditions, new technology and legislation affecting your industry.)
- The performance and vitality of your competitors

In this chapter you will develop a summary of this key information.

This is not a one-time analysis. Ideally you will look at market conditions annually to stay abreast of any changes and respond in a manner consistent with your brand.

The first step in this process is to look back at the last 12 months.

1. What were the greatest successes for your business in the last year?

_____

_____

_____

2. What were the major challenges your business faced in the last year?

3. Were there economic conditions in the region you serve that may have affected
   your business? What were they? What was their effect on your business?

## SWOT ANALYSIS

A SWOT Analysis is a deceptively simple tool used to identify and categorize all the significant factors that could positively or negatively impact your success. It allows you to look clearly at what will help you achieve your goals and what obstacles must be overcome to move forward. It breaks these into: internal issues (strengths and weaknesses) and external issues (opportunities and threats). Once categorized you will be able to analyze the factors that are present—or missing— that will help you achieve goals.

At first glance you may think: "I just did this in the last exercise." While they are similar, the scope of a SWOT analysis is broader and it focuses forward, unlike the last exercise, which was a review of the last year. That review gets you ready for a thorough and meaningful SWOT analysis.

### COMPLETE A SWOT ANALYSIS OF YOUR BUSINESS

| INTERNAL FACTORS | EXTERNAL FACTORS |
|---|---|
| Strengths | Opportunities |
| Weaknesses | Threats |

# WHAT FACTORS DEFINE THE SUCCESS OF A BUSINESS IN YOUR INDUSTRY

In any business, there are a few activities which are the primary determinants of success. If your company is especially good at these activities, your company will be successful.

These success factors usually fall into five categories:

1. **Strategic Focus.** This includes utilizing human and material resources so that you are flexible and nimble enough to take advantage of opportunities as they present themselves.

2. **Management and Development of People.** In a one-person business this means managing your own activities and development. This includes understanding motivation, providing direction, encouraging creativity and supporting personal growth.

3. **Business Operations.** This is really what people (you) do all day. This is the day-to-day fulfillment of your brand promise and giving clients what they want in the right way, at the right time and at the right price.

4. **Physical Resources** (which include facilities, finances and equipment). This is where the phrase "cash flow is king" comes in. It also means fitting the facility to the work. A manufacturer needs to have the right equipment in the right facility so there is economy of scale and safety is maintained for workers. A therapist needs a comfortable, safe space for clients—where their presence is confidential. (Some therapists even have clients enter and leave through separate doors so they can maintain the highest level of privacy.)

5. **Customer Relations.** This is central to success and includes branding, communications, marketing, and building and keeping relationships with clients. It is linked directly to strategic focus.

**List the key success factors that will make a difference for your business**

1. _____

2. _____

3. _____

4. _____

5. _____

6 _____

7. _____

8. _____

9. _____

10. _____

## COMPETITIVE FACTORS

Competitive factors set you apart from your competition. Common ones are listed in the example below. There are many others that may be unique to the market you serve.

| EXAMPLES | |
|---|---|
| What are the factors that set you apart from your competition? | Describe how these factors set you apart |
| Key Personnel | Third generation owner with sense of history and willingness to innovate |
| Management Structure/Organization | Strong leadership team |
| Level of Staff Expertise | Low turn-over and continuing education support develops staff into experts who are resources for customers |
| Quality | High quality compared to others who offer similar services |

| EXAMPLES | |
| --- | --- |
| What are the factors that set you apart from your competition? | Describe how these factors set you apart |
| | |
| | |
| | |
| | |
| | |

**COMPETITIVE ANALYSIS**

A competitive analysis is intended to provide information on several strategic factors:

1. What are your competitive advantages and how sustainable are they?

2. In the existing market for your business, what are the general characteristics of your key competitors?

Answers to these questions are essential to your understanding of your place in the market:

- What facts and assumptions exist about your key competitors?

_____

_____

_____

_____

- How can you validate these?

_____

_____

_____

_____

- What additional competitive advantage would this knowledge allow you?

_____

_____

_____

_____

In a strategically focused business, a competitive analysis is not a one-time occurrence; it is an ongoing task with a beginning, but no end.  Done properly, it provides key information to guide effective strategic decision-making with profitable results. This analysis is intended as a baseline, to be expanded with your own current and future knowledge as it is available.

A good understanding of a competitor's organizational structure, financial status, relative cost efficiencies and areas of expertise can provide significant guidance.  The benefits of collecting and using this data are numerous, enabling:

- Informed investment decisions and resource allocation
- The selection of market segments and effective brand positioning in areas where your competitors are not strong.
- Preparation of key competitive bids with winning results

There are three parts to a competitive analysis:

1. Collect information
2. Interpret and analyze the data (collected information)
3. Utilize what you learn in your strategic, communications and marketing plans

**COMPLETE A COMPETITIVE ANALYSIS FOR YOUR BUSINESS**

Who are your competitors? Choose 3 that are closest to what you offer and the clients you serve. Answer the following questions for each.

- What is their primary Market Segment?
- What are their Key Capabilities?
- What Strengths do they demonstrate?
- What Weaknesses do they show?
- What Opportunities do they have that they haven't yet taken advantage of (but may)?
- What Threats (internal and external) do they face?
- What Assumptions are you making about them when you complete this analysis?

COMPETITOR #1:

MARKET SEGMENT(S)

_____

_____

_____

CAPABILITIES

_____

_____

_____

_____

_____

OPPORTUNITIES

_____

_____

_____

_____

_____

STRENGTHS

_____

_____

_____

_____

_____

THREATS

_____

_____

_____

_____

_____

WEAKNESSES

_____

_____

_____

_____

_____

ASSUMPTIONS

_____

_____

_____

_____

_____

COMPETITOR #2:

MARKET SEGMENT(S)

_____

_____

_____

CAPABILITIES

_____

_____

_____

_____

_____

OPPORTUNITIES

_____

_____

_____

_____

_____

STRENGTHS

_____

_____

_____

_____

_____

THREATS

_____

_____

_____

_____

_____

WEAKNESSES

_____

_____

_____

_____

ASSUMPTIONS

_____

_____

_____

_____

COMPETITOR #3:

MARKET SEGMENT(S)

_____

_____

_____

CAPABILITIES

_____

_____

_____

_____

_____

OPPORTUNITIES

_____

_____

_____

_____

_____

STRENGTHS

_____

_____

_____

_____

THREATS

_____

_____

_____

_____

WEAKNESSES

_____

_____

_____

_____

ASSUMPTIONS

_____

_____

_____

_____

- Review all aspects of the information you have gathered on your competitors. What opportunities emerge for your business based on your discovery?

- Unserved or underserved populations that fit your client profile?

- Expansion into geographic areas not currently served?

- Products or services you provide that they do not? You may want to take advantage of some or all of these opportunities. However, just because there is an opportunity does not mean that taking the opportunity is the right thing for your business. This information will help you decide if you wish to do so.

OPPORTUNITIES BASED ON THE COMPETITIVE ANALYSIS

1. _____

_____

_____

_____

2. _____

_____

_____

_____

3. _____

_____

_____

_____

4. _____

_____

_____

_____

**NEXT STEPS TO TAKE ADVANTAGE OF OPPORTUNITIES**

The key question is, "What do I do now with all this information?" Sometimes more information can seem overwhelming. Having the data and evaluating how it relates to your business is sometimes enough. Seeing opportunities, as we have said, doesn't mean you must act on them. In fact, acting on them may not be in the best interest of your business—now or ever. It may be enough to have the knowledge.

The process of developing a competitive analysis often brings to light things you want to change, improve or track. As the last step in the process, determine any next steps that have emerged from this process. They do not need to be major changes—although they might be. Sometimes a small shift can give your business a significant boost.

**DESIRED CHANGES BASED ON THE COMPETITIVE ANALYSIS**

1. _____

2. _____

3. _____

4. _____

5. _____

6. _____

7. _____

8. _____

As we said at the beginning of the chapter, a competitive analysis is an ongoing process. This doesn't have to be an overwhelming addition to your to-do list. The initial process has given you a better understanding of where you and others most like you are in the market. This awareness will allow you to pay attention to your competitors in a more focused way. Each new bit of information you learn about them adds to your understanding of them and yourself.

## ONE LAST THOUGHT

The title of this book *Competition is Irrelevant* may seem at odds with this chapter. That couldn't be further from the truth. Understanding others who offer products/services similar to yours allows you to clarify what is unique about you and exactly who will benefit from what you offer. A competitive analysis can help you reach out to an underserved niche in the market and can illuminate the specific ways you can serve this niche that no one else currently is or can. In these ways you literally have no competition. In the next chapter we will look more deeply at Target Audiences and how to select and serve the one that is best for your business.

**NOTES**

CHAPTER 5

# TARGET AUDIENCE
## Do the right people know you are the right choice for them?

A tightly defined target market increases the ability of certain people to recognize themselves as part of that group. In order to facilitate that recognition among your best prospects, you need to define and understand your target market. In this chapter we will look at what a target market is and how you can define and refine yours so that you are truly engaging with the people you most enjoy working with and to whom you offer the most benefits and results.

## WHAT IS A TARGET AUDIENCE?

A target audience is a group of people you want to purchase your products or services.

The prospective clients in this target audience have many choices. They want to know why they should select you. As we saw in Chapter 3, being great at what you do isn't enough. Potential clients need to understand why you are the right choice for them. When people have an immediate, positive response to you and see what you offer as unique and of benefit to them they are more likely to choose you.

Your best clients are satisfied with your products/services, remain loyal, bring you repeat business and recommend you to others. These are your "on-brand" clients. What you offer matches what they need and want. They are attracted to you and understand how you are distinctive in what you offer.

### CONNECTING WITH YOUR TARGET AUDIENCE

#### UNDERSTAND WHAT YOUR TARGET CLIENT WANTS

1. Learn what they want and what they fear.
2. Understand the market climate for their business.
3. Determine how best to deliver a fulfilling experience for your clients.

## SHOW PROSPECTIVE CLIENTS WHY THEY SHOULD CHOOSE YOU

1.  Be clear about what you offer.

    - Tell potential clients what you will do for them.

    - Explain what they will get as a result.

2.  Showcase your value.

    - Focus on the benefits of working with you.

    - Define the solutions you offer to their business problems.

    - Connect your offer to their business goals.

3.  Define the response you want.

    - Encourage participation.

    - Offer an easy and clear path for engagement.

## FOLLOW THROUGH

1.  It's important that what you offer is clear—but it's even more important that everything you say and do delivers on what you promise.

2.  Staying true to your brand (keeping your promise) keeps your clients happy and builds a foundation for a lasting, meaningful, productive relationship with them. It keeps them coming back and makes you the one they recommend to their friends.

3.  Make sure your clients' experiences are consistent with your brand promise.

    - Are you fulfilling your brand promise with every client interaction?

    - What is it like for the client when you demonstrate your brand?

    - What are the essential actions you must take to deliver this client experience?

    - Do you currently have designated staff specifically tasked to deliver essential actions?

    - Does your business structure support the brand? If so, how? If not, what do you need to bring it into line?

# DEFINING YOUR TARGET AUDIENCE

Defining your target audience is somewhat counterintuitive. The common belief is that you want to make your audience as big as possible so you don't lose any opportunities.

In fact the opposite is true. When you narrow your target audience the people who will benefit the most from your products and services will see you as the right choice. In order to choose you they need to recognize that you benefit them and have a solution to their problem.

In Chapter 1 we discussed the traps people fall into when trying to appeal to a prospects:

- I'm excellent—I have great customer service
- I can do whatever you need—I can do that...
- I have the cheapest price in town

All of these traps widen the pool of people in your target audience...to include everyone, making any individual prospect less likely to understand why you are the right choice for them.

Almost everyone I've worked with says: "I have to appeal to everyone. I can't afford to turn anyone away."

In reality the more general you are, the less clear you are about the specific niche you serve. When people can say: "That's the niche I belong in," they are several steps down the road to selecting you.

Imagine that someone asks: "Who do you work with?"

You answer: "Women under 40."

That's so broad it means nothing. The person you are talking with probably won't sign up as a client or make any referrals to you.

Instead, you say: "I work with women in their 30s who are trying to advance their careers while raising children and maintaining a relationship. I coach these women on ways to build their careers and enjoy their personal life at the same time. I also write a blog that offers ideas to these women and provides a forum for them to connect with each other."

This description is much more likely to bring you clients.

## STEP 1: DEFINE YOUR NICHE

The first step in getting the right clients is to understand who you want to work with and why. Equally important is to know who don't you want to work with and why.

- Don't try to appeal to everyone.

- Define and focus on a specific market.

- Understand the characteristics of your ideal client; then look for potential clients with those characteristics. These include: personality, attitudes, values, interests and lifestyle.

- Don't be afraid to say no. The wrong clients won't build your reputation or your business but they will take your time and your energy away from the right clients.

Choose specific demographics to target. Determine not only who has a need for your product or service, but also who is most likely to buy it—and who you enjoy working with. Include the following factors. Skip to the next section if your target audience is other businesses.

Age _____

Location _____

Gender _____

Income level _____

Education level _____

Marital or family status _____

Occupation _____

## DETERMINE IF YOUR PRODUCT OR SERVICE WILL FIT YOUR TARGET MARKET

How and when will target clients use the product/service?

_____

_____

_____

_____

_____

What features are most appealing to them?

_____

_____

_____

_____

_____

How will my target client benefit from my product/service?

_____

_____

_____

_____

_____

What need will my product/service fill or problem will it solve?

_____

_____

_____

_____

_____

Are there enough people that fit my criteria to support my business?

_____

_____

_____

_____

Can my target client afford my product/service?

_____

_____

_____

_____

_____

## STEP 2: DEFINE YOUR IDEAL CLIENT

Who do you want to work with? Who are the best clients you've ever had? Who are your current favorite clients? This is the audience you want to talk with. Having a specialty that attracts your target clients insures that the right ones will find you.

- Understand the characteristics of your ideal client; then look for potential clients with those characteristics. These include: personality, attitudes, values, interests and lifestyle.

- Don't be afraid to say no. When you say, "I don't think I'm the right fit for you," it can save disappointment and lost time. Be helpful to prospects you turn down by offering them a referral or two for people you know who might offer a better fit.

RANK HOW IMPORTANT THE FOLLOWING CLIENT CHARACTERISTICS ARE TO YOU.
USE A 1-5 SCALE WHERE "1" IS LEAST IMPORTANT AND "5" IS MOST IMPORTANT

THE PERSON:

Knows what their problems and challenges are

| 1 | 2 | 3 | 4 | 5 |

Understands the benefits to finding a solution

| 1 | 2 | 3 | 4 | 5 |

Sees me as a valuable necessity rather than a necessary evil

| 1 | 2 | 3 | 4 | 5 |

Will tell friends and colleagues about me

| 1 | 2 | 3 | 4 | 5 |

Can pay me what I'm worth and will be happy to do so

| 1 | 2 | 3 | 4 | 5 |

Sees the benefits in learning and finding solutions

| 1 | 2 | 3 | 4 | 5 |

## DESCRIBE YOUR IDEAL CLIENT

Describe the person you do your best work with, who inspires you and leaves you feeling most energized

_____

_____

_____

_____

_____

How does this type of client allow you to be yourself?

_____

_____

_____

_____

_____

What is the problem or need of this target client?

_____

_____

_____

_____

_____

Are these problems I can solve for them?

_____

_____

_____

_____

_____

What functional value can I provide to this target client?

_____

_____

_____

_____

_____

_____

Describe the experience this person will have with me

_____

_____

_____

_____

_____

_____

# YOUR BRAND PROMISE

A Brand Promise is central to successful Brand Strategy because without it your brand is just a marketing gimmick.

*Know what you promise your clients—and then make sure that everything you say and do delivers on your promise.*

Keeping your promise makes your clients happy and builds the foundation for lasting, meaningful, productive relationships with them. It keeps them coming back and makes you the one they recommend or promote.

What do you offer your ideal clients? What do you promise you will do? What will they receive in return? Do they believe you care about them? Do they trust you to make their lives easier and less stressful?

## WHAT A WELL-CRAFTED BRAND PROMISE DOES

Successful brand promises are COMPELLING to potential clients. Your brand promise, your claims about your products or services, should be about something that your target clients care about. It also articulates what others fail to deliver or deliver less well.

CLEAR brand promises are the foundation of an effective marketing plan. The main purpose of a brand promise is to get customers to notice you and interact with you rather than others.

A clear brand promise inspires you and your employees to think creatively about your role and your involvement in delivering on your promise. It guides your decision making so you make better choices, more quickly. Decisions—hiring, who you target, what benefits you offer, what holiday card you send, what to wear to an important meeting—all based on your brand promise keep you on track and give clients a consistent and expected experience.

A clear brand promise is the first step in developing a marketing plan that works for you. It defines your target audience(s), formulates how to get their attention and how best to promote what you offer.

A brand promise must be CONCISE. The best brand promise needs no explanation. Every person who hears your brand promise will understand it. Your brand promise also needs to be easy to remember.

A successful brand promise is CREDIBLE. Today's consumers are acutely aware of the gap between what brands say and what they actually deliver. They are quick to abandon brands that fail to deliver what they promise.

Make sure that your brand promise is something you can DELIVER or your business will never succeed. Make sure that you never over-promise or under-deliver.

## HERE ARE SOME EXAMPLES:

### GEICO

"15 Minutes or Less Can Save You 15% or More on Car Insurance." Nearly everyone is familiar with this brand promise. Geico has made a huge investment in this campaign.

But catchy ads, the Geico gecko and a big ad budget are not what makes the Geico promise so compelling. It is memorable and believable because the promise is very specific. It quantifies not only what you will get (15% savings) but that you can achieve that in an easy, convenient way (takes only 15 minutes).[71]

### VIRGIN

The Virgin Group is made up of more than 400 companies, worldwide, including Virgin Atlantic, Virgin America and Virgin Mobile. The overarching brand promise across all Virgin companies is to deliver something better for consumers by shaking up the traditional, often boring, ways of doing things—reinventing through innovation and adding fun: as their website says, "We always aim to go beyond the norm to deliver unforgettable experiences for our customers."

Virgin America and Virgin Atlantic's in-flight safety videos reflect this brand promise. For a number of years they have offered entertaining videos that catch passengers' attention. They refresh these videos often so that they don't get stale.

In 2013 Virgin America's safety video was a highly produced music video. They described the video on their YouTube channel:

> Buckle up to get down. We've enlisted the help of Virgin Producer, Director Jon M. Chu, Choreographers Jamal Sims and Christopher Scott, Song & Lyrics by Todrick Hall, Composer/Producer Jean-yves "Jeeve" Ducornet, Virgin America teammates, and dance stars like Mike Song and Madd Chadd to give our safety video a new song and dance — literally. From the exit doors to the oxygen masks, no seat belt was left unbuckled.[72]

One flight attendant took this fun a step further. He commanded the attention of the passengers for all 5 minutes of the safety message when he danced along with the video as he demonstrated the safety tips.

Jameson Stafford who posted the video wrote in the description:

> *This video really shows the many shades of awesomeness of Virgin America. San Francisco to Los Angeles, late Friday Night, InFlight Team Leader, Mikey Tongko (Michael Tongko), rocks the whole plane during the pre-flight safety video. Dude is a dancing machine! Southwest, eat your heart out.*[73]

Others comments about this video on YouTube included:

> *"I never pay attention to the instructions, but, how can you NOT watch this? I would be transfixed. What a good beginning of a flight...."*

> *"I have been to some of the best flights in the world but they don't even have a safety video which is so full of joy and happiness in it. Usually safety videos be always like something like out of a drilling manual but this.... This is beautiful keep it up.*

> *"Been on a plane with him a few times before and he's always full of joy! Definitely the best flight attendant not just with VX, but all airlines I ever come across."*

> *"Even up in the air he genuinely comes across as a caring person who always keeps his cool even with some passengers who can really test ones patience. He always seems to find this great unique way of keeping everyone entertained all the time, every time."* [74]

Virgin is an excellent example of a brand that keeps its promise.

## DEFINE YOUR BRAND PROMISE

Define specifically what you promise your clients.

Be sure it includes:

- What you offer (in detail)
- What you will do/provide
- What your client will receive

Write down your Brand Promise

_____

_____

_____

_____

_____

Are you fulfilling your brand? Answering the following questions may help determine if you are or are not. Review your brand promise after you have answered these questions. You may want to tighten or change what you promise.

- What is it like for my client when I demonstrate my brand?

_____

_____

_____

_____

_____

_____

- What are they essential things I must do to deliver on this experience?

_____

_____

_____

_____

_____

_____

- What are the various ways I interact with my clients and that they experience my brand promise?

- How, specifically, am I fulfilling my brand promise in the various ways I interact with my clients?

- Does my business model support my brand? If so, how? If not, what do I need to do to bring it into line?

Review once again, "Am I fulfilling my brand promise and meeting the needs of my target audience?" If not, what immediate steps do I need to take to get back on track?

**NOTES**

## CHAPTER 6

# MAKING SURE YOUR INTERNAL HOUSE IS IN ORDER
## Keeping Your Brand Out of Trouble

## WHAT GETS A BRAND IN TROUBLE?

A brand is only as good as your ability to fulfill it. In this chapter we are going to look at a number of things that can—and often do—get in the way of developing and fulfilling a strong brand. Recognizing and understanding these Brand Pitfalls can help you can avoid them.

### COMMON PITFALLS

PIT·FALL NOUN\'PIT-,FOL\: A DANGER OR PROBLEM THAT IS HIDDEN OR NOT OBVIOUS AT FIRST.[75]

In Chapter 5 we introduced the importance of having a clear brand promise as the heart and soul of your brand. Many brand pitfalls are related to your brand promise so let's review the characteristics of a brand promise (from page 78).

A brand promise explains what you and your products and services will do for clients and what benefit they will receive as a result. A brand promise is also the expectation you create for yourself and your employees—something you and they can aspire to and achieve in your interactions with clients. While you create your brand promise internally, it is experienced externally.

- A successful brand promises is COMPELLING to potential clients.
- A CLEAR brand promise is the foundation of an effective marketing plan.
- A brand promise must be CONCISE.
- A successful brand promise is CREDIBLE.
- A brand promise is something you can DELIVER.

## PITFALL #1: NOT CLEARLY STATING YOUR PROMISE

### PROBLEM

If you don't tell people what you offer they will be confused and will have no idea what makes you special or how you can give them what they need and want. Your brand promise must be unique, compelling and believable to your target audience for them to take action by choosing you.

### CONSEQUENCES

- People don't know what you offer
- You don't stand out
- Market decides you promise something you don't
- Customers are disappointed
- People are confused

### BRANDS THAT CLEARLY STATE THEIR PROMISE

- Tom's of Maine: Tom's entered the market with the promise of all-natural ingredients which made them unique and compelling. They were distinct from both Crest and Colgate who both promised cavity and tartar control, making them hard to tell apart.
- Southwest Airlines defined its place in the market by offering no-frills flights at budget prices. By being upfront about what they offered—and what they didn't—they set themselves apart.

### HOW TO AVOID THIS PITFALL

- Know what you offer.
- You aren't like everyone else—know specifically how you are different from others.
- Create an easily understood—and memorable—description of what your target client will get and how they will get it.
- Quantify results (i.e. Geico's save 15% in 15 minutes).

## PITFALL #2: BREAKING THE PROMISE

### PROBLEM

Brands make promises to their clients in all phases of their relationship—prospect, new client, ongoing client. These promises can be explicit or more general statements of what to expect. To buy from you and to remain loyal and satisfied, people must have trust in you. They must believe you will do what you say you will. To gain their trust you must have integrity—consistently and predictably keeping your promise. High integrity leads to increased trust; breaking promises destroys trust.

### CONSEQUENCES

- Customers don't come back
- Customers are unhappy
- Loss of trust
- Risk of anger
- Negative word of mouth or negative reviews
- People choose someone else instead because they heard bad things about you
- Reputation is endangered

### TRUST AND INTEGRITY TOGETHER ARE A COMPETITIVE ADVANTAGE. THE OPPOSITE IS ALSO TRUE.

In spite of companies' good intentions and plans to follow through, a recent Accenture survey finds that an alarmingly high number of customers believe that companies regularly fail to keep their promises. According to the Accenture Broken Promises survey, a high proportion of Americans (40 percent) say the companies with which they do business made a promise to them in the past year and failed to keep it. Equally surprising, more than one-half (54 percent) of customers report that companies have broken multiple promises and believe companies are often unaware that this is happening.[76]

### HOW TO AVOID THIS PITFALL

- Focus on being a "promise keeper." Let it guide you through each day, each customer interaction and each activity.
- Ensure that you and your employees understand your brand promise and what it means to live it every day.

- Make sure every interaction with your clients and target audience expresses and fulfills your brand promise.

- Listen to your clients. Are their experiences consistent with your promise? If not, what do you need to do to bring their experience in line with your promise?

## PITFALL #3: MISALIGNMENT BETWEEN WHAT YOU PROMISE AND WHAT YOU DO

### PROBLEM

This is subtly different from breaking your promise although your clients' experiences may be very much the same. Saying the right thing is laudable. It loses all meaning if you do something else. I don't necessarily mean doing something bad or wrong. Just doing something different than you say you do. When clients hire you because they expect a certain thing but get something else, it doesn't matter how wonderful that something else is—your client will be disappointed.

In an interview with Business Insider on December 2, 2014, Jeff Bezos talked about the importance of brand clarity. "Paraphrasing [Warren] Buffett, Bezos said you could hold a rock concert. Or you could hold a ballet concert. But don't tell people they are going to a rock concert, then put on a ballet. Or conversely, don't tell people they are going to the ballet, then put on a rock concert."[77]

This misalignment comes from not clearly understanding your own brand promise and how it relates to what you do.

### CONSEQUENCES

- Customers are confused
- Customers don't know what to expect
- Customers are disappointed or angry
- Customers don't come back
- Customers don't recommend you
- You lose word-of-mouth opportunities

ADS VS. REALITY – FAST FOOD.

The blog Alphaila has an ongoing project, started in 2010, called: *Ads vs. Reality – Fast Food.*

The blog posts photos of fast food items as they are advertised and as they are actually sold. The difference is notable in every case.

> *False advertising 101. So, I went to some fast food places... I won't say "restaurants", just "places." After a lifetime of disappointment, bafflement, and frustration with the food, I decided it was time to do a little test, and compare the food you get with the ads. (I'm always on the hunt for little projects like this. Stoked.) I brought the food home, tossed it into my photography studio, and did ad-style shoots, with pictures of the official ads on my computer next to me, so I could match the lighting and angles.*[78]

We know that photos of food are carefully staged and photo-shopped—and sometimes what you see isn't really food at all. But these images on Alphaila are a stark illustration of the consequences of making false promises to customers. Go to their website: http://www.alphaila.com/articles/failure/fast-food-false-advertising-vs-reality/ to see the images. They are a reminder of how important it is to give your clients the products and experiences you have promised.

HOW TO AVOID THIS PITFALL

- Know what you promise.
- Understand what it means to keep your promise—not just theoretically— but how to put it into action.
- Review every communication you make—internally and externally— to ensure that you are doing what you promise.
- Ask clients for feedback and evaluate outcomes.
- Make sure you measure emotions as part of this. Clients can tell you if they are happy or unhappy—even if they can't tell you specifically why.

## PITFALL #4: NOT DISTINGUISHING YOURSELF FROM OTHERS

### PROBLEM

This occurs when you try to be like someone else—who usually has more visibility, experience or expertise—in order to gain credibility. This usually backfires because you aren't distinct and fade into the background. When you're trying to be someone else instead of yourself you can never be unique.

People respond to the distinctive things about you that they relate to. If you don't showcase those things you will get lost in a sea of others just like you.

### CONSEQUENCES

- You're easily overlooked
- People don't remember you
- Customers have no reason to go out of their way to choose you
- People revert to the choice with the lowest price

### WORDS MATTER

In *Brand Communication: Mind Your Brand Language*, Alistair Herbert and Ali Goode (Admap, 2014) report "Too many brands use generic words, making brand language repetitive and dull, but if they adopt a distinctive tone of voice and careful use of metaphors, they can own the words they put in the minds of their consumers."[79]

### HOW TO AVOID THIS PITFALL

- Clearly state what makes you unique.
- Find ways to be memorable.
- Make customers crave what you have to offer.
- Show through your actions.
- Define what is important to your target audience.

## PITFALL #5: CHANGING TOO OFTEN

### PROBLEM

Brands evolve to meet the need of their clients but a lack of consistency is confusing. Brand evolution works if it is done within the context of the brand promise when that promise is focused on the needs of a target audience and the mission of a company. Too much change is perceived as a bouncing ball. The client can't keep track of what the brand means.

### CONSEQUENCES

- People are confused
- Customers lose trust
- It is no longer clear that what you promise today will still be true tomorrow

### BRAND EVOLUTION VS. BRAND CONFUSION

On page 45 we looked at Starbucks' mission "to inspire and nurture the human spirit— one person, one cup and one neighborhood at a time." A Starbucks coffee shop on every block is common in cities around the world. In late 2014, Starbucks opened a roastery and coffee bar in Seattle that lets customers watch the whole roasting process while drinking their coffee. This new Starbucks roasts and serves premium coffees and boasts a Tom Douglas restaurant.

Rachel Lerman wrote in the *Puget Sound Business Journal*:

> *The roastery represents a major investment and focus on premium Starbucks Reserve coffee for the company. The 15,000-square-foot space will allow Starbucks to double its capacity for roasting the small-batch coffees. All Reserve coffee will be roasted at the Capitol Hill location and shipped around the world.*

> *Starbucks will open 100 new locations in the next five years around the world that sell only Reserve coffees. The feel of the new stores will be similar to the roastery — a bit fancier and more hipster than a standard Starbucks.*

> *"We are building a new brand within Starbucks," said Starbucks CEO and Chairman Howard Schultz at the company's investor day Thursday. "Very rarely do you get innovate and create within your core business."*[80]

The roastery was a passion and pet project of Schultz's for years, and he said the finished product "lapped every other retailer that you have possibly been to in your life."[81]

By contrast JC Penny, a major retailer for over a hundred years, nearly succumbed to this pitfall. Its merchandise was not unique—many items could also be found at Macy's, Walmart and Target. It used traditional retail sales methods to bring in customers: consistent stock, sales and coupons. Its customers were aging and the chain was not attracting younger buyers. As a result its sales were dropping. In 2012, new CEO, Ron Johnson, announced a major rebrand of Penny's. Based on his success at Target and the Apple Store, expectations were high.

Johnson implemented "everyday low pricing" and did away with sale pricing. The goal was to be more fair and consistent and build consumer trust. Unfortunately, his strategy backfired. With inadequate testing, Johnson didn't realize that the JC Penny core customer loved sales and coupons. It made them feel like 'smart shoppers.' Sales slumped. Research revealed the mistake and sales were reinstated—but not in the familiar ways core customers remembered.

Johnson also had a vision of a more modern, hipper, JC Penny that included boutiques and coffee bars within the store. These would attract a younger, more modern shopper. The reality was that this shopper stayed away and the old-fashioned shoppers couldn't find the merchandise or atmosphere they wanted. Sales staff who were comfortable in the old model didn't understand or want the new model. Johnson was fired in April 2013.

But by then, their core group of shoppers felt alienated, their new target shopper wasn't convinced and everyone was confused. Too many changes, too fast without a clear strategy left shoppers going elsewhere.[82]

## HOW TO AVOID THIS PITFALL

- Stay true to your mission and your brand promise.
- Evolution of your brand must be done carefully based on solid market research.
- Know what your target audience and core customer want and need.
- New product, services and sales methods must serve the needs of your audience.
- Change must be viewed, internally and externally, as a positive step that benefits the target audience and builds the brand.

## PITFALL #6: COMMUNICATING YOUR BRAND PROMISE IN THE WRONG WAY

### PROBLEM

Even when you have a strong brand promise and the ability to fulfill it with your clients, you still need to take one more step to attract clients. The character of the promise depends on your industry/sector. Using language that your target clients don't understand or doesn't fit their norms and personality won't resonate and may confuse or repel them.

### CONSEQUENCES

- People will ignore you
- You won't be believed
- Your target client will go elsewhere

### THE CHARACTER OF THE PROMISE

- If you are a tax attorney your target client will probably run other way if you promise them that your legal advice will be fun and make them feel happy (not a strong promise in any case, but you get the idea). Clients who are looking for legal advice on their taxes want someone who fully understands state and federal tax codes and will save them money. Fun isn't really what they are looking for. However, peace of mind would be.

- Businesses that market to consumers, on the other hand, often want to focus on fun and excitement. BMW *"The ultimate driving machine"* and Coca-Cola *"Open happiness"* elaborate their promises very differently, of course, but both deliver a "feel-good" promise. The promise is of a better, happier, more fulfilled life.

- In this and other service sectors and business-to-business the promise must be related to maximized value, fulfilling business needs and minimizing risk. If not there will be consequences.

### HOW TO AVOID THIS PITFALL

- Know who your target client is and what they want.
- State your promise so you showcase how you meet these needs.
- Use language and messages that reflect your industry and sector without resorting to jargon.

# DISCOVER AND OVERCOME YOUR PITFALLS.

List all the potential pitfalls that currently—or could potentially—affect your business.

List the steps you will take to mitigate or avoid each pitfall.

When you come across pitfalls in the future, use these pages to work through them.

| Pitfall | Current Pitfall | Potential Pitfall | What Steps to Mitigate? | Who Do I Need to Enlist to Help? |
|---|---|---|---|---|
| Not clearly stating your promise | | | | |
| Breaking your promise | | | | |
| Misalignment between what you promise and what you do | | | | |

| Pitfall | Current Pitfall | Potential Pitfall | What Steps to Mitigate? | Who Do I Need to Enlist to Help? |
|---------|-----------------|-------------------|-------------------------|----------------------------------|
| Not distinguishing yourself from others | | | | |
| Changing too often | | | | |
| Communicating your brand promise in the wrong way | | | | |

# INTEGRATE YOUR BRAND INTO EVERYTHING YOU DO, EVERY DAY

You've put together your brand strategy (Chapter 3). You understand the business climate that surrounds you (Chapter 4). You've determined your target audience (Chapter 5). You recognize potential pitfalls and have a plan to avoid them (Chapter 6).

It's time to take the next step and assess *how* you do business and ensure that everything you do fits your brand. This step is critical for business success and often overlooked.

Your brand is more than a marketing tool. It works most effectively for you when it's fully integrated into your business operations. It is important to look at each part of your organization for what is on-brand and off-brand.

Fair warning—you may have to make changes in how you do things. Generally, people try to avoid change. It isn't easy or comfortable. It's preferable to keep doing things the way we always have done them even if they are not working very well.

While it is better to determine when change is needed and embrace it, the first step in the process is to recognize our desire to maintain the status quo. Keep President Bill Clinton's comment in mind as you begin this process: *"The price of doing the same old thing is far higher than the price of change."*

## ARE YOUR BUSINESS PRACTICES ON-BRAND?

### PRODUCTS AND SERVICES

Your clients depend on you to provide a product or service that fulfills a need. They listen to what you promise and expect to receive value that fulfills that promise. It is important to answer these questions:

- List the ways your products/services are in line with your promise.

_____

_____

_____

_____

- What needs do your products and/or services fulfill?

_____

_____

_____

_____

_____

_____

- What needs could you fulfill for your clients that you don't currently with existing products and/or services?

_____

_____

_____

_____

_____

_____

_____

- In what ways do your products/services satisfy your clients and promote loyalty?

_____

_____

_____

_____

_____

_____

## TARGET MARKET

Your business and your clients evolve over time. It is important to periodically re-assess your target market and determine that you and they are still the best fit. Use your work in Chapter 5 to answer these questions.

- What is the profile of the right clients for both what you offer and how you offer it?

_____

_____

_____

_____

_____

_____

_____

_____

- Is this the client population you are currently serving? If not, why not?

_____

_____

_____

_____

_____

## TEAM AND CULTURE

No matter what your business structure—sole proprietor to large corporation—it is important to have people on your team who understand and promote your brand.

- Do you have the right people on your team (employees, contractors, consultants and vendors)? Describe the people on your team and the role each person plays.

_____

_____

_____

_____

_____

_____

_____

_____

_____

- List which team members best understand your brand.

_____

_____

_____

_____

_____

- Which team members best promote your brand? What methods do they use?

_____

_____

_____

_____

_____

## BUSINESS OPERATIONS

- Does your business operate in ways that are consistent with your brand?

_____

_____

_____

- Do your operations focus on your customer relationships and fulfilling your brand promise?

_____

_____

_____

## MARKETING CAPABILITIES AND PERFORMANCE

Marketing plans must be both focused and flexible. They are most successful when they are driven by Brand Strategy. Marketing plans need occasional revisions to adapt to your clients' needs. Be careful of changing too much which may make you appear indecisive or insecure in what you offer. It is important to keep these decisions consistent with your brand.

- Is your marketing plan up-to-date and in-line with your brand strategy?

---

---

---

---

- How are you tracking the effectiveness of your marketing efforts? One way to do this is to track if prospects are converting to clients.

---

---

---

---

---

---

---

---

---

---

# PRACTICES NECESSARY TO CONDUCT BUSINESS ON-BRAND

## ACME CONSULTING

Acme is a small fictional recruitment process outsourcing company. It handles 100% of its clients' recruiting functions, including all sourcing and hiring functions as well as exit strategies when employees leave the organization.

Acme's consulting services allow their clients' organizations to run more efficiently because they will have the right talent in each job position, they will always have the optimum number of employees and staff shortages will be fixed before they become major problems.

## ALIGN YOUR BUSINESS ACTIONS

A strong brand organizes your internal actions and distinguishes you to the outside world. The goal is to align each action with it so that it fulfills your brand promise and positioning strategies. (See Acme Consulting example on next page.)

Take a look at the assessment you just completed of your business practices. Which of these practices/activities are on-brand and which ones are off-brand?

ON-BRAND:

- _____
- _____
- _____
- _____
- _____

OFF-BRAND:

- _____
- _____
- _____
- _____
- _____

| Acme's Brand Promise | On Brand | Off Brand |
|---|---|---|
| Personalized service that is customized to the client's needs | Meets the key staff at the client office frequently and uses effective listening skills to assess what is needed now or may be needed in the future. | Visits the client's office only when there is a problem. |
| | Not only knows the job description for each position in the company but also knows each person and their strengths and challenges. | One size fits all approach. Uses standardized job descriptions for the industry as a guide. |
| | Determines the client's desired level of engagement in the hiring process and proceeds accordingly. | Has a process that is used for all clients. |
| Two steps ahead at all times | Uses social media as a recruiting tool. Sources talent through community contacts. | Has a file folder of talent that is updated annually. |
| | Keeps up with the company's successes and obstacles so that talent is sourced to fit their current and future needs. | Relies on the information gathered in an intake questionnaire to determine the needs of the company. |
| Staff shortages fixed before they become major problems | Utilizes information gathered from ongoing communication with clients to anticipate their staffing needs and suggest strategies proactively. | Responds to client requests for staff recruitment as needed. Responsibility is placed on the client to determine when help is needed. |

## CHANGE WHAT'S OFF-BRAND TO ON-BRAND

Start by determining 1-3 activities that are the most important to the success of your business.

For each one state your desired outcome and outline the steps—based on your brand strategy—you will take to get there.

**BUSINESS PRACTICE #1:**

_____

_____

Desired Outcome

_____

_____

_____

_____

Plan

_____

_____

_____

_____

**BUSINESS PRACTICE #2:**

_____

_____

Desired Outcome

_____

_____

_____

_____

Plan

_____
_____
_____
_____

**BUSINESS PRACTICE #3:**

_____
_____

Desired Outcome

_____
_____
_____
_____

Plan

_____
_____
_____
_____

Next, define the 5 things you need to do to make sure everyone in your business understands and lives your brand.

1. _____

2. _____

3. _____

4. _____

5. _____

What 7 things do you need to do to align your company activities with your brand?

1. _____

2. _____

3. _____

4. _____

5. _____

6. _____

7. _____

What are 3 ways you will build your brand into your business goals and objectives?

1. _____

2. _____

3. _____

At what point do you want to have everyone associated with your business activities aligned with the brand promise?

_____

_____

_____

_____

What things will be in place that let you know that you are there?

_____

_____

_____

What are the 6 most important benchmarks for getting there?

1. _____

2. _____

3. _____

4. _____

5. _____

6. _____

The exercises in Chapters 3-6 have led you through the development of your Brand Strategy. Now we turn our attention to the communication of your Brand to your target audience—your current clients and prospective clients. Chapter 7 will give you a structure for doing this.

**NOTES**

_____

_____

_____

_____

_____

_____

_____

**NOTES**

CHAPTER 7

# BRAND COMMUNICATION
## Define Yourself: Attractive and Distinctive

Now that you have defined your brand strategy and are aware of potential pitfalls—
and how to avoid them—it's time to share your brand with others. This is simple—and
multifaceted—at the same time. In order for prospective clients to find you attractive
and distinctive you need to find the best ways to connect with their hearts and minds.
Let's break down how people engage with you.

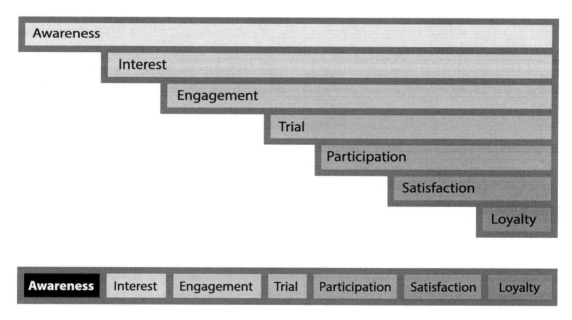

Brand awareness and recognition are built on communication that is consistent, effective
and facilitated by understandable verbal and visual triggers. These include your business
name, tagline, brief description of what you do, key visuals (logo, font, colors) as well as
memorable experiences with you.

The world we live in is a noisy, busy place. People have lots of choices. Being different
is one way to stand out. But being different isn't enough. You have to demonstrate your
difference and make it easy for your target audience to understand that difference.

People also need to understand that you are good at what you do. It's not enough to say it. But it's great if other people say it about you. Testimonials, reviews and word of mouth all give third party credibility to what you do.

## TO DO'S:

- Decide the best ways to get in front of *current clients*. What do you want them to know about why they are benefitting from choosing you? How will you communicate with them most effectively?

_____

_____

_____

_____

_____

_____

_____

_____

_____

- Decide the best ways to get in front of *potential clients*. What do you want them to know about why they will benefit from choosing you? How will you communicate with them most effectively?

_____

_____

_____

_____

_____

_____

_____

_____

_____

- Review the strategies you currently use to increase the familiarity and recognition of your brand. Put together a plan based on what currently works and what needs adjustment.

_____

_____

_____

_____

_____

_____

_____

- Take advantage of market opportunities. Develop strategies that allow you to be nimble and effective when you see market opportunities.

_____

_____

_____

_____

It isn't enough to be noticed. You have to make people curious to know more. People want to understand what you do. They want to know who you are. They also want to know what's in it for them.

Chris Flett, founder of Ghost CEO™, has three questions he tells people they must be able to answer before they let their market know that they exist:

1.  What do I do?
2.  Why does it matter?
3.  Who cares?

*Since 1999, I've been using the three questions as a major foundation piece of the Ghost CEO™ model. In that time, I have talked to literally tens of thousands of entrepreneurs around the globe and you know how many have been able to answer the three questions well on the first or fourth try? Zero. Not one. Nobody. Nada . . . If they can't answer the questions well, they will only ever compete in the market on price . . .* [83]

Your personality attracts others to you. We gravitate to individuals, companies and products that we judge to have similar personality traits to ours. One reason it is so important to define your target audience is that attraction based on personality is a two way street. We want to attract clients who are attractive to us. Review your three top personality traits from Chapter 3 to see what prospects may be looking for in you.

## TO DO'S:

**Answer Ghost CEO's questions:**

* What do I do?

_____

_____

_____

_____

_____

- Why does it matter?

_____

_____

_____

_____

_____

- Who cares?

_____

_____

_____

_____

Share your answers with 3 people (friends, family, colleagues or champions). Ask for their reactions and record them here:

_____

_____

_____

_____

_____

_____

_____

_____

| Awareness | Interest | **Engagement** | Trial | Participation | Satisfaction | Loyalty |
|---|---|---|---|---|---|---|

It is important to engage with people emotionally. People think with their heart and their guts. Facts, figures and rationales are important, but if you start there you will quickly lose people's attention. People want to laugh and cry and even worry a little bit. They want you to tell them why they should care. They want to feel connected to your story. This is what draws people in and keeps them there.

> *Emotional Branding is the conduit by which people connect subliminally with companies and their products in an emotionally profound way. Google's innovation, France's romance, Gucci's sensual elegance, Vogue's iconic glamour, and Tiger Wood's amazing drive and spirit reach us emotionally by striking our imaginations and offering promises of new realms. This strategy works because we respond emotionally to our life experiences and we naturally project emotional values onto objects around us.*[84]

The essence of engagement is relationship. This means connection not transaction.

## TO DO'S:

- Assess how you are providing compelling and unique client experiences that go beyond a specific product or service. Record your methods here.

- Define what emotions connect you and your target audience.

Commitment is difficult. Few people want to jump in right away. People seek meaning. They want to see what you stand for. They want a way to test the waters—to see if they like what they experience before they commit. They are looking for two elements: honesty and trust. Honesty is an expectation; trust must be built.

At the trial stage people are looking for indications they can trust you. They may read your website, attend a presentation you give, "window shop" without buying anything, read an article you wrote or someone wrote about you. They are looking, assessing but not yet buying.

People who are interested in you also want to know that you are interested in them. More than that, they expect you to know them and understand what they need. However, having a product or service that meets their need is not enough. People want experiences that fulfill their desires. These "wants" are often largely intangible. They are about the how rather than the what. When people try you out, they are looking for fulfillment from the experience.

## TO DO'S:

**Review your Brand Assets from Chapter 3 to see what will attract your prospects.**

- Make sure all your business decisions are rooted in your brand. Business strategies that are consistent with your brand prompt your clients to action—action that you define and that builds your business. Record whether this is happening and if not how you will remedy it.

- List how you show clients and prospects your interest in them.

- What methods do you use to determine if your clients and prospects trust you? If you do not have methods in place, establish a timeline for developing them. Record that here.

If the trial went well the person is ready to sign up. At this point they believe that you offer expertise and excellence. They trust you to give them what they need. This is a critical point where it is essential that they find consistency in their experience with you. Fulfilling your brand promise is key. When you fulfill your brand promise in every interaction, it gives people the security they need to remain in relationship with you.

Cultivate the relationship with your clients by building a partnership characterized by open communication and personal connection. Client relationships have the same characteristics of a friendship: honesty, sensitivity, generosity, humor, support and a willingness to listen.

## TO DO'S:

- Define the essence of your relationship with your clients.

- Determine what role you want to play in your client's life.

| Awareness | Interest | Engagement | Trial | Participation | **Satisfaction** | Loyalty |

You made a promise. You fulfilled it. Your client knows what to expect, receives it and finds value in it. Your client now prefers you to others.

At the Awareness stage you sought to be Known. At this point you are Preferred and striving to be Loved.

People understand you, value what you offer and return each time because they felt fulfilled in your last interaction. As long as you are clear about your brand promise and consistently fulfill it, your clients will remain satisfied.

## TO DO'S:

- What are 3 to 5 things you did or can do to make sure your clients are satisfied?

- Ask for client feedback. Create a structure for this so it is consistent across clients.

- Remain open to new ways of meeting clients' needs rather than offering products and services that no longer have value to your best clients.

When your client stays with you they are loyal. They are in it for the long haul because you offer them something they value and their experience of that is consistent over time.

Loyal clients become your champions by recommending you to others. Because they understand and appreciate you they advocate for you and what you offer. They are your secret weapon. John Jantsch, in his book, *The Referral Engine*, tells us that humans' brains are hardwired to make referrals. This is because, "The hypothalamus likes validation—it registers pleasure in doing good and being recognized for it, and it's home to the need to belong to something greater than ourselves. This is the social drive for making referrals." [85]

## TO DO'S:

- Reward loyalty. Whether this is a loyalty program or unexpected thank you notes or small gifts, it is always well received. What do you do now? How do you know whether it's effective?

_____

_____

_____

_____

_____

_____

_____

_____

- If you don't currently reward loyalty, devise a plan to do so. Record your plan here.

_____

_____

_____

_____

_____

_____

_____

_____

_____

Think about your most loyal clients. What traits do they have in common?

- _____

- _____

- _____

- _____

- _____

- _____

- _____

- _____

- _____

- _____

List 5 indicators that will let you know your clients are loyal

1. _____

_____

2. _____

_____

3. _____

_____

4. _____

_____

5. _____

_____

Invite your loyal clients to become champions. Develop a plan for doing this and record it here.

_____

_____

_____

_____

_____

_____

_____

_____

_____

_____

_____

_____

_____

_____

# WHAT TO SAY AND HOW TO SAY IT

It's time now to turn your focus outward and start a conversation with your clients and prospects that will grow over time and enhance your relationship with them.

The first step is to translate your brand into messages that are understandable, accessible and persuasive. If you don't communicate in a way that your target audience understands, they will never believe you are what they want and need.

## 3M CORPORATION

Post-it® and Scotch® tape are among the most well-known of 3M's vast array of products. Their brand revolves around the company's focus on innovation and invention rather than focusing on its products.

> *3M is a global innovation company that never stops inventing. Over the years, our innovations have improved daily life for hundreds of millions of people all over the world. We have made driving at night easier, made buildings safer, and made consumer electronics lighter, less energy-intensive and less harmful to the environment. We even helped put a man on the moon. Every day at 3M, one idea always leads to the next, igniting momentum to make progress possible around the world.*[86]

3M publishes their *Identity Strategy & Policies* on their website. Included is a *Message to Employees and Suppliers*.

> *Across languages, cultures and diverse markets, people around the world come to know 3M products and services through our brand. In more than 190 countries, the 3M brand identity is realized through a powerful, unifying strategy for communicating the value, trust, leadership and ingenuity behind our brand. When 3M is consistently recognized for these characteristics, we build our familiarity and market leadership. This, in turn, increases the value of our brand, bringing benefits to all of our businesses.*[87]

3M also lists their key messages with the following introduction.

*Key messages are created to help describe who 3M is and what solutions we offer, both in words and images. Key messages are not intended to be used word-for-word. Instead, they are to serve as guides, and as the foundation for expressing 3M's distinct personality and tone.*

*Below you will find key messages that support our company (the foundational elements of our philosophy and structure as a diversified technology company) and our brand (the messages that leverage our brand promise and essence to connect external audiences with the power of the 3M "authority" brand underlining innovation).*

*3M is a diversified technology company.*

*3M applies innovation systematically to anticipate and respond to customer needs.*

*Practical and ingenious solutions are a strong part of 3M's legacy.*

*3M is a global company with presence throughout the world.*

*3M consistently fulfills its commitment to investors, customers, employees and communities.*

*3M fosters a culture of leadership at all levels.*[88]

## DEVELOP YOUR KEY MESSAGES

Before you start this exercise review your mission, guiding principles, brand assets (see Chapter 3) and brand promise (See pages 80-83). Next review your target audience (see pages 71-77). Imagine you are speaking directly to a person in your target audience. Use language you know that person will understand.

- What is the most important thing this person needs to know about what you can do for them?

- Describe what you can do for them—the benefits of working with you.

 

- How are you different from others in your field or industry?

 

- Why do you want to work with this person?

- Describe what the themes and messages mean for your target audience.

_____

_____

_____

_____

_____

_____

_____

_____

## YOUR STORY

The next step is to take these key messages and put them together in a story that can serve as the basis for a variety of communications with clients: one-on-one, your website, marketing materials, social media and advertising. It will give you consistency and clarity as you reach out to your target audience.

Create the story with the client in mind, using your key messages:

- Tell the most important things first and then create a path through the story that pulls the listener along.
- Draw the listener into the story through emotional connections.

Story telling is part of human nature. Stories have been present in cultures around the world throughout time. Stories create emotional connection, teach and preserve culture.

Stories are memorable in part because they have a recognizable structure. In the beginning we are introduced to the characters, the location and the situation or problem. The characters experience growth and change in the middle section of the story. The end of the story provides resolution—whether happy or tragic.

_In a landmark 1944 study, 34 humans — Massachusetts college students actually, though subsequent research suggests they could have been just about anyone — were shown a short film and asked what was happening in it. The film showed two triangles and a circle moving across a two-dimensional surface. The only other object onscreen was a stationary rectangle, partially open on one side._

*Only one of the test subjects saw this scene for what it was: geometric shapes moving across a plane. Everyone else came up with elaborate narratives to explain what the movements were about. Typically, the participants viewed the triangles as two men fighting and the circle as a woman trying to escape the bigger, bullying triangle. Instead of registering inanimate shapes, they imagined humans with vivid inner lives. The circle was "worried." The circle and the little triangle were "innocent young things." The big triangle was "blinded by rage and frustration."*[89]

People understand and expect this story arc. It is present in novels, plays, movies, fairy tales, songs and even abstract cartoons. Joseph Pulitzer, the famous editor, said, "Put it before them briefly so they will read it, clearly so they will appreciate it, picturesquely so they will remember it and, above all, accurately so they will be guided by its light."

This is the essence of brand communication.

## TEN ESSENTIAL STEPS IN CREATING YOUR STORY

1. Start with your listeners in mind. Who are they? What do they care about? How can you offer them something of value—both in the moment and in a longer relationship?

2. First step – engage your audience. Start with an interesting anecdote or a surprising fact about you. Weave the key points of your story into a conversation. That means listen as much as you talk. Show an honest and sincere interest by asking questions and commenting on what they say.

3. Use language that resonates with your listeners/readers. You want others to hear what you have to say, understand it and pass it on to others.

4. Find your own voice and use it consistently so people will recognize it as part of who you are. Make sure you are resonant and impactful while remaining real and truthful.

5. Make each element of your story easy to understand. Distill to the essence. Less is more. Make your story clear, brief and precise. We live in a world with many distractions so you need to get to the point quickly. While we tend to roll our eyes about the fast pace of communication, the reality is that people are used to 140 character tweets and media sound bites.

6. Make each statement memorable. This makes you more recognizable and it's easier for others to pass on your story to others.

7. Be persuasive. Not in-your-face or demanding but rather engaging, compelling and credible. Lead with your benefits—why you matter rather than your features.

8. Avoid robotic recitation of your story. If you tell your story in a way that indicates that this is the 1,001st time you've told it your audience will be as bored as you sound.

9. People can only really remember three things. Make sure you communicate the most important three things it a way that is understandable and memorable.

10. End with a call to action. What do you want the person to do now that they've heard the story? Be specific.

## STORYTELLING NOW

The year 2012 was seen as "the year of the story" in marketing. Brands sought to develop compelling, amusing, emotional stories that were told across all channels of communication.

While sharing through social media was growing exponentially, stories were still being told by presenting messages to an audience.

Today telling stories is no longer the same. The process of developing a story remains the same but delivering stories has changed. It's no longer enough to tell others what you think they should know. Conversation—listening, sharing and finding connection—is now an integral part of your story.

The best communication makes people feel that you are talking directly with them, no matter where or how you share information. The goal is to create a conversation. This means sharing information and listening at the same time—the way you do in an engaging, compelling social conversation.

Today, sharing online enables people to share more information—from more sources—with more people—at an accelerated pace.

The New York Times Customer Insight Group published a study, *The Psychology of Sharing: Why Do People Share Online*. Their key finding was that online sharing is all about relationships.

They outlined the key motivations for people to share:

- To bring valuable and entertaining content to others
- To define ourselves to others
- To grow and nourish our relationships
- Self-fulfillment
- To get the word out about causes and brands
- To bring valuable and entertaining content to others
- To define ourselves to others
- To grow and nourish our relationships
- Self-fulfillment
- To get the word out about causes and brands

The study sites 7 Key Factors that influence sharing:

1. Appeal to the consumers' motivation to connect with each other—not just with your brand
2. Before people will share your story, they must trust you and believe your story is true
3. Keep it simple...and it will get shared...and it won't get muddled
4. Appeal to their sense of humor
5. Embrace a sense of urgency
6. Getting content shared is just the beginning (get shared—get shared again—listen—get credit for responding—respond)
7. Email is still #1[90]

There are more online platforms every day. Wordpress reported in October 2014 that "Over 409 million people view more than 16.3 billion pages each month. Users produce about 61.8 million new posts and 55.4 million new comments each month."[91]

The consumer decides where and with what to engage. What attracts is content. Social media is about story; it is about connection; it is about emotion. We share stories across social media. Stories "go viral" based on their ability to engage, shock, amuse and inform.

# YOUR STORY

## WRITE YOUR STORY

As you write your story, think of who you want to engage as you develop your story. Think about the conversation you are starting.

Before you start writing, check off who needs to know your story?

- ❏ Customers and Prospects
- ❏ Industry Experts
- ❏ Members of Professional Associations you belong to
- ❏ Strategic Partners
- ❏ Vendors
- ❏ Your Employees
- ❏ Your Board of Directors/Shareholders
- ❏ Investors/Financial Community
- ❏ Media
- ❏ The General Public
- ❏ Competitors (You're not like anyone else. They can be allies rather than enemies.)
- ❏ Others

Make sure your story has a beginning, middle and end. Tell the most important things first and then create a path through the story that pulls the listener along. Outline your story here—you will write a full version later in the chapter:

_____

_____

_____

_____

_____

_____

_____

_____

_____

_____

Answer the question: "How will using my product/service make your life easier or better or what problem does it solve?"

_____

_____

_____

_____

_____

_____

_____

Where and how will you tell your story?

_____

_____

_____

_____

_____

_____

_____

_____

Who will pass your story on to others?

_____

_____

_____

_____

_____

_____

**WRITE YOUR STORY HERE.**

_____

_____

_____

_____

_____

_____

_____

_____

_____

_____

_____

_____

_____

*Competition is Irrelevant*

Review your story to make sure you have included the following and revise it as needed.

— Connect with people's emotions:

  • People want to laugh and cry and even worry a little bit.

  • They want you to tell them why they should care.

  • They want to feel connected to your story.

  • This is what draws people in and keeps them there.

— Utilize the tools you've developed:

  • Your Brand Promise

  • How you are Unique, Memorable, Believable and Important

  • Your Personality

  • A Positioning Statement

  • Key Messages

— End with a call to action:

  • What do you want the person to do now that they've heard the story?

  • Tell them—be specific.

  • Tell them more than once—before you tell the story and at the end.

These exercises will set the stage for how the world sees you. We will discuss this more in Chapter 8.

**NOTES**

_____

_____

_____

_____

_____

_____

**NOTES**

# CHAPTER 8

# HOW THE WORLD SEES YOU
## Brand Image

Brand image is the way you are perceived by your target market—a set of thoughts, feelings and beliefs they hold about you. Brand image is written—spoken—visual—tactile—subliminal—overt—conceptual—and literal. All these influence what people think about you and your brand. This chapter will provide a brief overview of the components of a brand image and how to make it happen.

Remember, your clients are not just choosing your product/service—they are choosing the brand image they perceive. For some that comes before full knowledge of what you offer. You want your brand image to be positive, immediate and unique.

| PERCEPTION | POSITIVE | IMMEDIATE | UNIQUE |
|---|---|---|---|
| **What Not To Do** | Don't tell people what you want them to think about you—show them what you are. | Don't make people stop and think about who you are, what you offer and what sets you apart. Make it immediately obvious. | Don't try to match what others are doing or saying. This just makes you part of the crowd—people won't see you or understand why you are the best choice for them. |
| **What To Do** | Interactive communication is the key to keeping your brand image positive. Show who you are by engaging, listening and demonstrating. | Use logos, taglines and other things associated with your brand to prompt recognition. When people see/hear/feel repeatedly they recognize you automatically in the back of their mind. | You want to stand out in people's minds. Remind people what makes you different and how that benefits them. When you first understand what sets you apart you can then demonstrate those qualities in all your business activities. This allows you to showcase your uniqueness. |

*"In order to be different, one must always be different."*
*- Coco Chanel*

## WHAT CONTRIBUTES TO YOUR BRAND IMAGE

The first step is to ensure that the things that contribute to your brand image are well thought out. These fall into three categories: Clarity, Benefits and Consistency.

### CLARITY

A clear brand personality is recognizable and memorable. People understand who you are and how you are different from others in your industry.

What makes you recognizable, memorable and distinct? (Refer to the Brand Asset exercise in Chapter 3.)

_____

_____

_____

_____

_____

_____

_____

_____

_____

_____

_____

_____

# BENEFITS

Benefits cause people to choose you over others. There are three kinds of benefits:

## FUNCTIONAL BENEFITS

- What you do better than anyone else
- How you can help clients achieve their goals

## EMOTIONAL BENEFITS

- Shared values
- Perceived similarities
- Ways you make clients feel good

## RATIONAL BENEFITS

- Your believability
- How you will help clients resolve concerns or problems

## DEFINE YOUR BENEFITS.

(The Brand Assets and Personality you defined in Chapter 3 will help you identify these.)

1. The functional benefits I provide:

_____

_____

_____

_____

_____

_____

_____

_____

_____

2. The emotional benefits I provide:

_____

_____

_____

_____

_____

_____

_____

_____

_____

3. The rational benefits I provide:

_____

_____

_____

_____

_____

_____

_____

_____

_____

_____

_____

## CONSISTENCY

Your brand image must be consistent to be effective. Our world is a busy, noisy place where people have many choices. Consequently, brands clamor for attention. In order to stand out your image needs to be consistent. Consistency helps turn down the noise and calm the busyness.

As people become familiar with you they recognize you more quickly. The triggers for recognizing your brand image include:

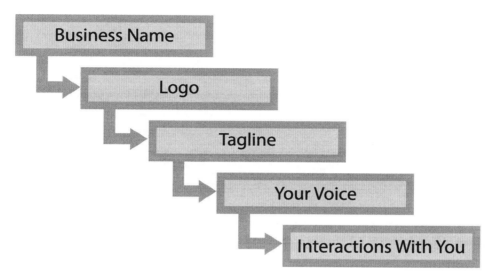

## BRAND ASSOCIATIONS

What do we mean by Brand Associations? They are the elements that represent your brand and that people interact with through their senses: what they can see, hear, feel, smell and sometimes taste. They are often the face of your brand to the outside world.

People learn to associate these elements with your brand. Associations are important—very important—because they catch people's attention, connect with them emotionally, and remind them who you are. They are tools that communicate your brand—literally, shortcuts that trigger your audience's memories about you.

Brand associations—name, logo, tagline, color palette, visual images, website, social media, advertising, packaging, public relations campaigns—strengthen and enhance your brand.

Often, brand associations are so representative of the brand that they are considered the brand. That is why, when we think; "I need a brand," it is natural to want to immediately create a great name, an amazing logo, a business card and a website.

When we think of big brands we tend to think of them in terms of their logo, name, tag-line or key visual. Everyone knows Nike's slogan: "Just Do It." When we see Golden Arches, we think McDonald's. The NBC Peacock has had many design iterations to reflect the trends of the time, yet the concept of the Peacock is timeless.

*Let me say once again, it is important to define your brand strategy and get your business practices in order before you choose your name and logo.*

We don't think about the fact that a brand image is the end result of a branding process and there are many layers—the ones we have addressed in previous chapters—that underlie the development such an image.

The remainder of this chapter will briefly outline the major elements of a brand image. This is in no way an exhaustive enumeration of the possible components of a brand image.

Having done your homework in the preceding chapters you are ready to decide what brand association will work most effectively for you. It is important to take the time to determine what is needed to best reach your target audience. Are they online most of every day? Then a website is essential with associated social media and possibly a blog. Do they commute to work? Then advertising on buses, billboard or on the radio may be most appropriate.

Most people are not prepared to develop their brand associations on their own. While choosing a business name and tagline may be within your skill set, designing a logo or a website may not be. You want these to be polished and professional. It is better to have only the key pieces—and these well done—than to have all the elements look like your kid did them. I highly recommend hiring a professional to help you translate your brand strategy into unique associations.

The following exercises and examples will prompt your thinking before you undertake the development of your brand image.

## NAME

A perfect name is unique, defines what is offered as premium, explains what the product or service is and what it does. Unfortunately, the perfect name rarely (if ever) exists.

Names fall into one of five categories:

1. Generic names describe the product or service and are not unique. They also cannot be trademarked.

   *Example: lawyers.com*

2. Descriptive names are literal and tell you exactly what is offered.

   *Examples: Three-Day Blinds, Bed 'N Breakfast Registry*

3. Suggestive names use metaphor and analogy to create emotional reactions and positive connections.

   *Examples: Greyhound Bus Lines, Amazon*

4. Arbitrary names are real words used out of context.

   *Examples: Apple, Windows*

5. Fanciful names are made-up. They may sound like real words but aren't found in the dictionary.

   *Examples: Verizon, Kodak, Exxon*

## NAME YOUR BRAND

1. Start with a description of your business. How would you describe it to someone who knows nothing about it? You have about 10 seconds to engage the person and another 20 seconds to fill out the picture.

2. Use your description to help you brainstorm as many words as possible—
descriptive or made up—that are:

- Emotionally evocative

- Experiential

- Have sensory associations

    - Visual

    - Auditory

    - Touch

    - Smell

    - Taste

3. Now play with the words you've written down. Combine them. Expand on them. Find
related words. Go for volume; 40-50 is not too many. Put each one on a note card and
begin shuffling them. Take some out. Add some new cards that have combinations of
two or more.

As you play with the cards, try to think like a potential client. Remember your name
helps bring awareness of your business, creates interest in what you do, is the first step
in the engagement process and oftentimes helps people decide to try you out.

4. Put the cards down and go do something completely unrelated. Maybe wait a day or two. Come back to the cards and choose your top ten. Make sure you are pleased with the group of ten, but don't let yourself fall in love with any of them yet. Make sure the name is easy to say and easy to spell. List them here.

_____

_____

_____

_____

_____

_____

_____

5. Do the research. Search for the name online and pay close attention to what you find. Check if it has a trademark. Is it the domain name for a website? Quickly eject any that are already taken or too generic.

6. Add more names and do the research until you have 5 names. List them here.

1) _____

2) _____

3) _____

4) _____

5) _____

7. Test the 5 names. Ask friends, family, colleagues what they think. For each name ask them:

   • What does this company do?

   • What emotions does the name elicit?

   • Does it make you want to learn more about the company and what it offers?

8. Assess the responses.

    - If you have a winner—congratulations!  Go to step 9.

    - Be ready for them to all be duds. This happens! It's part of the process and doesn't mean anything negative.  If you need to, go back to step 2 and redo the process. Use any resources you want: surf the net, pull out the dictionary or the thesaurus and reread everything you've written about your company.

9. Create the domain name. It should be as close to the brand name as possible. It's best to choose a .com or .org name (anyone can register a .org domain but it is best used for a non-profit, foundation, institute, etc.). If someone else has the .com name, DON'T use the name with .biz or dot anything else. We are trained to think that everything is a .com.

10 Use the name. Say it out loud—a lot. Insert it into your marketing materials. Go away for a day and come back and read them. Do you still like the name? Love the name? When you are sure go to #11.

11.  Trademark your name. Then tell the world.

## TAGLINES

A tagline is a short phrase or series of words that capture the essence of a brand—its personality, purpose and character. They are deceptively simple. The process of creating a tagline requires introspection, research and feedback from friends, colleagues and stake-holders.

Examples of well-known, successful taglines:

| | |
|---|---|
| Target | "Expect More. Pay Less." |
| YouTube | "Broadcast Yourself" |
| Dairy Council | "Got milk?" |
| Olay | "Love the skin you're in" |
| Allstate Insurance | "You're in good hands with Allstate" |
| Kellogg's Frosted Flakes | "They're gr-r-r-eat!" |
| Disneyland | "The happiest place on earth" |
| Las Vegas | "What happens here, stays here" |
| The Container Store | "Contain Yourself" |

## CREATE YOUR TAGLINE

Creating a tagline is a process of trial and error which often includes dashed hopes and valleys of despair. The best advice is don't rush and don't give up.

Before you start, go back to chapter 3 and reread your mission, vision, guiding principles, values, brand assets and personality. Think also of the benefits you provide clients.

- Using these as a guide, brainstorm words that reflect who you are. Remember, your name and tagline must work together.  Brainstorm lots and lots of ideas.

- Write them all down here.

- Leave them alone for a day or two and reread them. Select the ones you still like. Write them here.

Select your top 3-5. For each one answer the following questions:

1.  Is it memorable, believable and unique?

2.  What benefits does it offer?

3.  What emotions does it elicit?

**Tagline #1:**

1.  Is it memorable, believable and unique?

_____

2. What benefits does it offer?

_____

_____

_____

_____

3. What emotions does it elicit?

_____

_____

_____

_____

**Tagline #2:**

1.  Is it memorable, believable and unique?

_____

2. What benefits does it offer?

_____

_____

_____

3. What emotions does it elicit?

**Tagline #3:**

1. Is it memorable, believable and unique?

2. What benefits does it offer?

3. What emotions does it elicit?

**Tagline #4:**

1. Is it memorable, believable and unique?

2. What benefits does it offer?

3. What emotions does it elicit?

**Tagline #5:**

1. Is it memorable, believable and unique?

2. What benefits does it offer?

3. What emotions does it elicit?

Review all 5 taglines and select the one that best represents you.

## LOGO

A logo is a visual image associated with your business. It is the basis of your corporate image. It is recognizable because it is consistent everywhere it is seen.

It takes a special set of skills to translate brand strategy into an image that communicates through the use of signs and symbols, so again consider hiring a professional.

A logo can be abstract, pictorial, word based. The most effective logos tell the story of your business in one or two concepts. Logos rarely stand-alone but often are so well known they instantly connect with the company, product or service.

While not all logos contain hidden messages, a surprising number include a treasure to be discovered that enhances the meaning and makes the logo even more memorable.

Examples of logos with hidden messages.

An arrow is hidden between the E and x suggesting speed of delivery.

NBC has one of the most easily identified logos. The white space in the center is a peacock.

The "G" in the name Goodwill is a smiling face that reflects the face in the logo.

**PITTSBURGH ZOO**
**& AQUARIUM**®

When you look closely at the tree you can see the silhouette of a gorilla on the left and a lion on the right. At the bottom, three fish are jumping.

The ball is the wheel of a bicycle.
The "R" is a bicyclist leaning over the wheel.

## EMPTY VESSELS

Names, taglines and logos can be "empty vessels." That means that they hold very little meaning on their own. The meaning is developed over time through marketing campaigns, customer experience and word of mouth. When the element is memorable and it is paired with a quality product it can become iconic.

## COLOR PALETTE

What color says about your brand is more complex than you might think. Everything else can convey the message you are trying to send only to be undermined by colors that are unpleasant or send a completely different message than the intended one. Knowing your audience, understanding the meaning of colors and looking at them in relationship to each other are all important factors. Engaging a graphic design professional is the safest way to get it right.

## TYPOGRAPHY

Typography also sends subtle and subliminal messages. Which fonts to choose, what combination of fonts, how many fonts, spacing and color all contribute to a congruent message with your logo and other design elements? When you get it right, most people won't really notice. When you get it wrong, they will feel something is off, even if they can't define what it is. This is another place where a graphic designer can help you.

## BUSINESS CARDS AND OTHER COLLATERAL

Brand collateral is the set of online and printed materials that tell your story. Included are letterhead (printed and electronic), brochures, envelopes, websites, Facebook and Twitter designs, ads, signs and point of sale materials.

All pieces of your collateral need to be coherent and provide meaning and authenticity. They represent you and your business. Their job is to remind others who you are and what you offer. They are what people recognize before they realize they have recognized you.

A well-crafted business card is one of the single most important ways to convey your brand. It never goes out of style even if some industries and for some consumers, the business card is less common than the electronic sharing of contact information.

## WEBSITE

A website is no longer optional and no longer confined to the desktop. To be most effective in reaching your target audience you need a website that is clean, experiential and well organized with content that is easily accessible and highly visual. It must be available—and usable—across all platforms: desktop, laptop, tablet, phablet and phone. This means it must have a responsive template that automatically optimizes the website content layout for the device that it is being displayed on.

The web architecture and navigation must be simple to use and instantly accessible. The graphic design must be consistent with your brand and the content must be simple to access quickly but comprehensive enough to explain what you offer.

Steve Krug in Chapter 1 of his book *Don't Make Me Think! A Common Sense Approach to Web Usability* (second edition) suggests the most important feature of any website:

> *Don't make me think! I'VE BEEN TELLING PEOPLE FOR YEARS THAT THIS IS MY FIRST LAW OF USABILITY. And the more Web pages I look at the more convinced I become.*

*It's the overriding principle—the ultimate tie breaker when deciding whether something works in Web design. If you have room in your head of only one usability rule make it this one.*

*It means that as far as humanly possible, when I look at a Web page it should be self-evident. Obvious. Self-explanatory.*

*I should be able to 'get it'—what it is and how to use it—without expending any effort thinking about it.[92]*

## SOCIAL MEDIA

Social media is the fastest growing part of a marketing plan.

Historically, information went one direction—from the organization to the consumer. Organizations listened to customers only through formalized methods such as focus groups.

### OLD MODEL OF COMMUNICATION

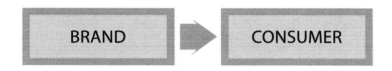

Now, online channels allow consumers to be an active part of the conversation—they build the brand through their networks. Consumers compare and discuss information about you and your competitors who offer the same or similar services. It is very important to listen to consumers. What are they are saying about you? What are they saying about your competition? What questions do they have?

Your goal is to develop and maintain long-term, meaningful, productive relationships with your clients.

Social media instantly increases your online exposure. It increases your search engine optimization (SEO): online activity makes you rank higher in search engine results. Links posted from your website direct traffic back to your site and also rank higher due to activity.

# NEW MODEL OF COMMUNICATION INFLUENCED BY SOCIAL MEDIA

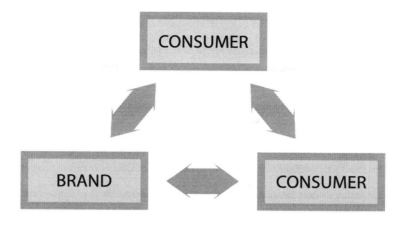

## SOME COMMON MISCONCEPTIONS ABOUT SOCIAL MEDIA

### SOCIAL MEDIA TAKES TONS OF TIME AND ENERGY

There are strategies and tools that help manage your social media. For example, you can schedule Facebook and Twitter posts in advance to save time.

### THERE ARE SO MANY DIFFERENT SOCIAL MEDIA CHANNELS—I CAN'T DO THEM ALL

You really don't need to do them all. Select the platforms that make the most sense for sharing your content. Facebook is better for businesses talking to consumers. Use Twitter if you know your target market frequents it. LinkedIn is best for connecting with a large network and is considered the social media channel for business. Pinterest and Instagram work when you are sharing pictures and other visual images.

Consider working with a professional who can help you decide what platforms are best for you.

**DESIGN YOUR SOCIAL MEDIA STRATEGY**

1. What is your objective?

_____

_____

_____

2. What do you want to say?

_____

_____

_____

_____

3. What platforms are you going to use?

_____

_____

_____

_____

4. How are you going to build relationships and community?

_____

_____

_____

_____

_____

5. Who is going to manage your social media activities?

6. How often will you post?

7. How will you stay on target?

8. How are you going to measure progress and success?

# STANDARDS AND GUIDELINES

Designing a visual brand identity that truly represents you takes a lot of time and energy. As we have discussed, consistency is one way you can increase your audiences' recognition of you and remind them what you offer.

 Imagine if the Twitter logo was different every time you saw it: a different color, facing a different direction, or not used at all. The average person would understand this was still Twitter but it would take longer to "get it". The ideal identity is positive, immediate, and unique which translates into consistent.

## BRAND IDENTITY GUIDELINES

To achieve consistency you need brand identity guidelines. If your brand isn't consistently portrayed and communicated your entire brand promise and story are compromised. It results in lack of recognition and brand confusion.

Creating a Brand Identity Guidelines Manual gives you and everyone who works with you—staff, graphic designers, printers, and consultants—the information to keep things clear and consistent. It ensures that your brand image is not distorted, improves your marketing efforts and keeps you focused.

A Brand Identity Guidelines Manual is a written document that explains how your brand identity will be used internally and externally. Its role is to define the rules of consistency for the visual elements of your brand. It provides very specific instructions about how tangible elements of your identity will be used. By following these guidelines, your brand will become more immediately recognizable and more memorable.

Comprehensive brand guidelines include instructions about colors, fonts and layout. These are used in business papers, signage, ads, printed materials, website and social media.

Typically, your graphic designer produces your Brand Identity Guidelines Manual for you.

### CONTENTS OF YOUR BRAND IDENTITY GUIDELINES MANUAL

#### 1. Brand Overview

Your manual starts with an overview of your brand. This is a summary of the information you developed in Chapter 3. It focuses on your Brand Promise and includes your values, guiding principles and key messages.

## 2. Logo and Tagline

Your logo is the most tangible visual element of your brand identity. It is important to define exactly how it will be used. Included in this are color and black and white versions, where your logo will be positioned in different materials; size and space around the logo.

## 3. Trademarks and Intellectual Property

If your business owns specific trademarks or intellectual property, you may be required by law to use specific wording or styling in your branded communications. Include when a trademark symbol (™) or registered mark (®) is required after your brand name.

## 4. Color Palette

This includes primary, secondary and tertiary colors with their specific Pantone (PMS) colors. It defines when and how to use each color. It also includes the RGB, HEX and CMYK equivalents of your PMS colors. If you don't know what all these letters mean, ask your graphic designer.

## 5. Typography

This is a full definition of all the fonts you use in all online and printed communications. It includes font size, line height, kerning and any other customization of the fonts. You may have to use different fonts for online vs. printed materials. Be sure to include these differences.

## 6. Imagery

These are photos and images beyond your logo. It is important to think in advance about what is on-brand and what is off-brand.

## 7. Voice

It is important to maintain a consistent voice in all your written or spoken communications. Instructions related to formal/informal, everyday/professional/technical is helpful.

## KEEP YOUR MANUAL UPDATED

This is essential and will simplify your life.

Share your Brand Identity Guidelines Manual with everyone who works with you—staff, graphic designers, printers and consultants. It is the key to clarity and consistency. Don't risk brand confusion by failing to remain consistent.

**NOTES**

*Competition is Irrelevant*

## CHAPTER 9

# IS YOUR BRAND WORKING FOR YOU?
## Evaluating Your Brand and Its Effectiveness

If you are reading this final chapter and you have completed all the exercises in all the chapters leading up to this one—congratulations. You have built a brand that will enhance your visibility and credibility. You understand what makes you unique and who you are best suited to work with. You know how you want to communicate with your best clients and prospects and you know what you want to say.

You now have a brand that will work for you—if you let it. The worst thing you can do at this point is put this book back on the shelf thinking, "I've done that and now I'm finished."

Your brand does nothing for you if it sits on that shelf. Your brand is the face of your business to the world. It is a resource for making effective business decisions about your products/services and how to manage your business functions.

Your brand gives you a structure for evaluating your strategy and communications so use it to deliver on your promise and ensure your clients continue to get exactly what they need—from you and you alone.

## A BRAND THAT EVOLVES STAYS FRESH AND CURRENT

Everything changes: trends—fashion—language—methods of communication— the economic climate—technology—politics.

As the world changes you may find your products/services slowly moving out of style or even becoming obsolete. Brands that don't keep up become irrelevant and eventually disappear.

Strong brands are built on a mission to solve problems for a certain kind of person. If your brand is all about a specific product or service you risk failure.

Polaroid is a prime example of a company that focused on producing a specific product rather than giving customers a way to achieve certain goals.

Polaroid sought to bring something different to photography—instant photography. Early in its history it appealed to artistic photographers. Its film had qualities that enhanced film as an artistic medium. In the 1970s, Polaroid began to appeal to the mainstream photographer who wanted to have fun and be spontaneous.

As digital photography grew, the need for instant film deceased. Digital became the new fun photography and the mainstay for those who need quick photography for their work. Industries who needed instant photos no longer had to deal with film at all.

Polaroid didn't offer anything to either of these groups because they stayed with film instead of moving to digital. The consequence for Polaroid was loss of market share and a collapse of their business.

The Polaroid experience highlights how important it is to listen to your target audience and join them in conversation. The difference between what the market wants now and what it will need in the near future can be great or small but it rarely stays the same.

When you add, adapt, update and anticipate the products and services that will serve your target audience while staying true to your mission, you remain relevant and stay ahead of what your market needs.

If a business finds itself in this situation, it must rebrand to regain attention of its market and remain relevant to its target audience. Unfortunately, rebranding often fails. Businesses wait too long and then try to take too big a leap to catch up. Brand promises get confused and communication gets muddled. Remember the Pitfalls in Chapter 6. These pitfalls loom large in a rebrand.

All the principles of Brand Strategy come into play in keeping your business evolving and relevant.

## STAYING ON TOP OF YOUR BRAND

Your brand is an asset that needs to be protected, preserved and nurtured. This requires a disciplined approach to analyzing the quality of what you offer and its success in meeting the needs of your target audience.

It is very helpful to perform periodic evaluations of how well your brand is working. An annual evaluation is the minimum. You may want to review these questions quarterly or semi-annually.

As you go through this list you will see that many of the questions are ones you pondered in earlier chapters. Since you've just completed the process of building your brand it's not time to conduct a review. For now, read through the questions, decide when you want to complete the evaluation and put it on your calendar.

## BRAND REVIEW

### HOW WAS THE LAST 12 MONTHS FOR MY BUSINESS?

- How much did my sales increase (or decrease)?

<br><br><br><br>

- Are more people aware of me and what my business offers? If you said "yes," how do you know this? Can you quantify this increase?

<br><br><br><br><br><br>

### ARE YOU WORKING WITH THE RIGHT CLIENTS?

Take a look at your client list for the last year. Are you serving the people you had in mind or the people that showed up? We all want to build our businesses. So, it makes sense to say "yes" when someone wants to work with us. If you aren't careful, you will have a list of clients who are "off-brand." They take energy away from your best clients and don't build your business.

**Using your client list, answer the following questions:**

- The next step is to identify your best clients—usually about the top 20% of all your clients.

_____

_____

_____

_____

_____

- What makes them the best?

_____

_____

_____

_____

_____

**KEEPING MY BEST CLIENTS.**

- What value do I deliver to my best clients?

_____

_____

_____

_____

_____

- Which of my clients' problems do I solve?

_____

_____

_____

_____

- What customer needs am I satisfying?

- What products and services am I offering my clients?

- Are my best clients happy with every interaction they have with me? If yes, how do I know? If no, what can I do to insure all interactions meet their approval?

- Do I regularly check in with my best clients to gauge their satisfaction? If "yes," how do I do this and how often do I do it?

_____

_____

_____

_____

- If I haven't checked in regularly, what can I do going forward to assess their satisfaction?

_____

_____

_____

_____

## BECOMING VISIBLE TO A LARGER AUDIENCE.

- What strategies will get me in front of more prospects?

_____

_____

_____

_____

_____

_____

_____

- How can I showcase what my business offers so prospects understand what I do and why it's important to them?

_____

_____

_____

_____

_____

_____

_____

- How do I build relationships with potential clients?

_____

_____

_____

_____

_____

- How can I make my messages more consistent and effective?

_____

_____

_____

_____

_____

- Are all my marketing materials consistent with my key messages? If no, when can I rework my marketing materials?

_____

_____

_____

_____

_____

## TAKING ADVANTAGE OF MARKET OPPORTUNITIES.

- What new audiences could benefit from what I offer?

_____

_____

_____

_____

_____

- What new products or services could I offer my current clients?

_____

_____

_____

_____

_____

- What resources would I need to take advantage of new opportunities?

_____

_____

_____

_____

_____

_____

- How can I stay true to who I am (my brand) if I expand?

_____

_____

_____

_____

_____

## ONE FINAL THOUGHT

The integrated brand that you have developed by completing this workbook is a powerful tool for your business. It guides you, supports you, and showcases what you offer. Use it as a resource for making business decisions and developing your strategies. Use the tools you have developed in the workbook to deliver on your promise and ensure your clients continue to get exactly what they need—from you and you alone.

## *When you are branded properly, competition is irrelevant.*

**NOTES**

# CHAPTER 10
# ENDNOTES

## FOREWORD

## CHAPTER 1

1. LePla, F. Joseph, Susan V Davis and Lynn M Parker. Brand Driven: The Route to Integrated Branding Through Great Leadership. London and Sterling, VA: Kogan Page, 2003. XIV. Print.

2. Zmuda, Natalie. "Pepsi Tackles Identity Crisis." 7 May 2012. Advertising Age. 5 March 2015 <http://adage.com/article/news/pepsi-tackles-identity-crisis/234586/>.

3. Tuttle, Brad. Two Ways McDonald's Is Trying to Win Over Millenials. 11 September 2014. 7 March 2015 <http://time.com/money/3327751/mcdonalds-millenials-mcbrunch/>.

4. McDonald's. McDonald's USA Announces New Brand Division. 2 January 2015. 15 March 2015 <http://news.mcdonalds.com/US/news-stories/McDonald-s-USA-Announces-New-Brand-Vision/>.

5. WARC. McDonald's leverages marketing layers. 27 January 2015. 8 March 2015 <http://www.warc.com/LatestNews/News/EmailNews.news?ID=34216&Origin=WARCNewsEmail&CID=N34216&PUB=Warc_News&utm_source=WarcNews&utm_medium=email&utm_campaign=Warc-News20150127/>.

6. Enterprise Rent-A-Car. Find Car Rental Locations by City in the United States. 2012. 7 March 2015 <http://www.enterprise.com/content/car_rental/popularLocations.html>.

7. Enterprise Rent-A-Car. Enterprise Rent-A-Car Customer Replacement Rentals. 2008. 7 March 2015 <http://www.enterprise.com/content/car_rental/replacement-rentals.html>.

8. Enterprise Rent-A-Car. Enterprise Rent-A-Car Customer Replacement Rentals. 2008. 7 March 2015 <http://www.enterprise.com/content/car_rental/replacement-rentals.html>.

9. Forbes. Enterprise Holdings on Forbes America's Largest Private Companies List. October 2014. 8 March 2015 <http://www.forbes.com/companies/enterprise-holdings/>.

10. Nordstrom. About Nordstrom. 2015. 7 March 2015 <http://shop.nordstrom.com/c/about-us/>.

11. Nordstrom, Bruce A. Leave It Better Than You Found It. Seattle: Documentary Media, 2014. 109. Print.

12. Nordstrom, Bruce A. Leave It Better Than You Found It. Seattle: Documentary Media, 2014. 110. Print.

13. PressReader. Protect Your Image. 18 February 2015. 25 March 2015 <http://www.pressreader.com/south-africa/the-mercury/20150218/281535109428331/TextView/>.

14. Klein, Naomi. No Logo: Taking Aim at Brand Bullies. Tenth Anniversary. New York: Picador USA, 2009. 4. Print.

15. Poterba, James M. Tax Policy and the Economy. Cambridge: MIT Press, 1999. 9. Print.

16. USA Today. After 25 years, 'Just Do It' remains iconic tagline. 21 August 2013. 25 March 2015 <http://www.usatoday.com/story/sports/nba/2013/08/20/nike-just-do-it-turns-25/2679337/>.

17. Nike. About Nike. 2015. 25 March 2015. <http://about.nike.com/>.

18. Meyers, Jack. Adbashing: Surviving the Attacks on Advertising. Parsippanyu, New Jersey: Amer Media Council, Inc., 1993. 39. Print.

19. The Washington Post. 25 Years of AOL: A timeline. 2010 May 23. 25 March 2015 <http://www.washingtonpost.com/wp-dyn/content/article/2010/05/23/AR2010052303551.html>.

20. LoginRadius. Social Media: Where it's been, where it's going. June 2014. 25 March 2015 <http://blog.loginradius.com/2014/06/social-media-evolution/>.

21. Internet Live Stats. Total number of websites. 2015. 25 March 2015 <http://www.internetlivestats.com/total-number-of-websites/#trend>.

22. Web Deisgn Depot. A Brief History of Blogging. 14 March 2011. 25 March 2015 <http://www.webdesignerdepot.com/2011/03/a-brief-history-of-blogging/>.

23. Petronzio, Matt. A Brief History of Instant Messaging. 25 October 2012. 25 March 2015 <http://mashable.com/2012/10/25/instant-messaging-history/>.

24. Prssa, Emu. A Forefather of Social Media: Andrew Weinreich and SixDegrees.com. 26 May 2012. 25 March 2015 <http://emuprssa.com/2012/05/26/a-forefather-of-social-media-andrew-weinreich-and-sixdegrees-com/>.

25. Internet Live Stats. Total number of websites. 2015. 25 March 2015 <http://www.internetlivestats.com/total-number-of-websites/#trend>.

26. Middleton-Moz, Jane and Mary Zawadski. Bullies, Revised: From the Playground to the Boardroom. Deerfield, FL: Heath Communications, Inc, 2014. 109. Print.

27. Stoll, Clifford. Why the Web Won't Be Nirvana. 26 February 1995. 8 March 2015 <http://www.newsweek.com/clifford-stoll-why-web-wont-be-nirvana-185306/>.

28. Statista. Number of monthly active Facebook users worldwide as of 4th quarter 2014 (in millions). 2015. 8 March 2015 <http://www.statista.com/statistics/264810/number-of-monthly-active-facebook-users-worldwide/>.

29. Internet Live Stats. Total number of websites. 2015. 8 March 2015 <http://www.internetlivestats.com/total-number-of-websites/#trend>.

30. YouTube. Statistics. 2015. 8 March 2015 <http://www.youtube.com/yt/press/en-GB/statistics.html>.

31. Twitter. About Twitter. 2015. 8 March 2015 <https://about.twitter.com/company/>.

32. Statista. Number of worldwide internet users from 2000 to 2014 (in millions). 2015. 8 March 2015 <http://www.statista.com/statistics/273018/number-of-internet-users-worldwide/>.

33. Fox, Susannah and Lee Rainie. The Web at 25 in the U.S., About This Report. 27 February 2015. 8 March 2015 <http://www.pewinternet.org/2014/02/27/summary-of-findings-3/>.

34. Apple, Inc. Apple Reinvents the Phone with iPhone. 9 January 2007. 8 March 2015 <https://www.apple.com/pr/library/2007/01/09Apple-Reinvents-the-Phone-with-iPhone.html>.

35. Apple, Inc. Apple Launches iPad. 27 January 2010. 8 March 2015 <https://www.apple.com/pr/library/2010/01/27Apple-Launches-iPad.html>.

36. O'Dell, Jolie. For the First Time, More People Get News Online Than From Newspapers. 14 March 2011. 8 March 2015 <http://mashable.com/2011/03/14/online-versus-newspaper-news/>.

37. Holcomb, Jesse, Jeffery Gottfried and Amy Mitchell. News Use Across Social Media Platforms. 14 November 2013. 8 March 2015 <http://www.journalism.org/2013/11/14/news-use-across-social-media-platforms/>.

38. Pew Research Center. Mobile Technology Fact Sheet. January 2014. 8 March 2015 <http://www.pewinternet.org/fact-sheets/mobile-technology-fact-sheet/>.

## CHAPTER 2

39. Eells, Josh. Most Creative People 2014. June 2014. 8 March 2015 <http://www.fastcompany.com/3029211/most-creative-people-2014/anna-kendrick/>.

40. Berscheid, E. and E. H. Walster. Interpersonal Attraction. Reading: Addison-Wesley Publishing Company, 1969. 73. Print.

41. Heider, Fritz. The Psychology of Interpersonal Relations. Psychology Press, 1958. Print.

42. Heider, Fritz. The Psychology of Interpersonal Relations. New York: John Wiley & Sons, 1958. Print.

43. Heath, Chip and Dan Heath. Made to Stick: Why Some Ideas Survive and Others Die. New York: Random House, 2007. 246. Print.

44. Heath, Chip and Dan Heath. Made to Stick: Why Some Ideas Survive and Others Die. New York: Random House, 2007. 14. Print.

45. Wegner, David. Do You Make Buying Decisions Based on Logic or Emotion? A Tale of Two Chickens. 21 April 2010. 8 March 2015 <http://www.today.mccombs.utexas.edu/2010/04/do-you-make-buying-decisions-based-on-logic-or-emotion-a-tale-of-two-chickens/>.

46. Landman, Anne. BP's "Beyond Petroleum" Campaign Losing its Sheen. 3 May 2010. 8 March 2015 <http://www.prwatch.org/news/2010/05/9038/bps-beyond-petroleum-campaign-losing-its-sheen/>.

47. Aenlle, Conrad. BP Stock: 5 Reasons to Ignore the Plunge and Take the Plunge. 2 June 2010. 8 March 2015 <http://www.cbsnews.com/news/bp-stock-5-reasons-to-ignore-the-plunge-and-take-the-plunge/>.

48. Bakewell, Sally. BP to Sell U.S. Wind Business in Retreat to Fossil Fuels. 3 April 2013. 8 March 2015 <http://www.bloomberg.com/news/articles/2013-04-03/bp-to-sell-u-s-wind-buiness-in-retreat-to-fossil-fuels/>.

49. Velvet Tissue. Our New TV Advert. 2015. 8 March 2015 <http://www.velvettissue.com/our-new-tv-advert/>.

50. Young, Laurie. How to Foster Brand Loyalty Effectively. December 2011. 8 March 2015 <https://www.warc.com/Content/Documents/A95955_How_to_foster_brand_loyalty_effectively.content?PUB=BESTPRAC&CID=A95955&ID=4348bd2e-e0f9-44bb-9d20-69235d49efe3&q=&qr=>.

51. Schultz, Howard and Dori Jones Yang. Pour Your Heart Into It: How Starbucks Built a Company One Cup at a Time. New York & Boston: Hachette, 1997. 248. Print.

52. Freeman, Karen, Patrick Spenner and Anna Bird. Three Myths about What Customers Want. 23 May 2012. 8 March 2015 <http://blogs.hbr.org/2012/05/three-myths-about-customer-eng/>.

53. Herbert, Alastair and Ali Goode. Brand communication: Mind your brand language. May 2014. 8 March 2015 <http://www.warc.com/Content/Documents/A101755_Brand_communication_Mind_your_brand_language.content?PUB=ADMAP&CID=A101755&ID=357e143b-cfa3-4896-9ac2-481fe2462b57&q=&qr=>.

54. Herbert, Alastair and Ali Goode. Brand communication: Mind your brand language. May 2014. 8 March 2015 <http://www.warc.com/Content/Documents/A101755_Brand_communication_Mind_your_brand_language.content?PUB=ADMAP&CID=A101755&ID=357e143b-cfa3-4896-9ac2-481fe2462b57&q=&qr=>.

55. Cunningham, Alice. "Olympic Hot Tub Company's Use of Their Website and Blog to Build Customer Relationships" E-mail interview. 5 March 2015.

56. Adamson, Brent, et al. The End of Solution Sales. July 2012. 8 March 2015 <https://hbr.org/2012/07/the-end-of-solution-sales/>.

57. Luke, Darla. Getting Lost on the Internet. 22 September 2012. 8 March 2015 <https://seejanepublish.wordpress.com/2012/09/22/getting-lost-on-the-internet-by-darla-luke/>.

58. Laird, Sam. Taco Bell Comes up With Another Epic Social Media Win. 3 January 2013. 8 March 2015 <http://mashable.com/2013/01/03/taco-bell-epic-social-media-win/>.

59. Taco Bell. 8 March 2015 <https://www.facebook.com/tacobell/>

## CHAPTER 3

60. Google. Ten things we know to be true. 2015. 8 March 2015 <http://www.google.com/about/company/philosophy/>.

61. Whole Foods. Our Core Values. 2015. 8 March 2015 <http://www.wholefoodsmarket.com/mission-values/core-values/>.

62. Microsoft. Microsoft Accessability Mission, Strategy, and Progress. 2015. 8 March 2015 <http://www.microsoft.com/enable/microsoft/mission.aspx>.

63. Schultz, Howard. An Open Letter from Howard Schultz, ceo of Starbucks Coffee Company. 17 September 2013. 8 March 2015 <http://www.starbucks.com/blog/an-open-letter-from-howard-schultz-ceo-of-starbucks-coffee-company/1268>.

64. Microsoft. Microsoft Accessability Mission, Strategy, and Progress. 2015. 8 March 2015 <http://www.microsoft.com/enable/microsoft/mission.aspx>.

65. Starbucks. Mission Statement. 2015. 8 March 2015 <http://www.starbucks.com/about-us/company-information/mission-statement/>.

66. Microsoft. Human Rights. 2015. 8 March 2015 <http://www.microsoft.com/about/corporate citizenship/en-us/working-responsibly/principled-business-practices/human-rights/>.

67. Starbucks. Business Ethics and Compliance: Standards of Business Conduct. 2011. 4 April 2015. <http://globalassets.starbucks.com/assets/eecd184d6d2141d58966319744393d1f.pdf>.

68. Cattell, Heather E.P. and Alan D. Mead. The Sixteen Personality Factor Questionnaire (16PF). 1946. 10 March 2015 <http://central.rcs.k12.tn.us/Teachers/cowartg/16PF%20Cattell.pdf>.

69. Ali, Syed Wajahat. Five Factors of Personality. 6 April 2012. 8 March 2015 <http://docslide.us/documents/the-five-factors-of-personality.html>.

70. Aaker, Jennifer L. "Dimensions of brand personality." Journal of Marketing Research 34.3 (1997): 347-356.

## CHAPTER 4

None

## CHAPTER 5

71. Geico. Genies: Did You Know - Geico. 3 November 2014. 8 March 2015 <https://www.youtube.com/watch?v=Colw-GucKw0&list=PL139A69A037F3A12D/>.

72. Virgin America. Virgin America Safety Video Dance #VXsafetydance. 29 October 2013. 8 March 2015 <https://www.youtube.com/watch?v=DtyfiPIHsIg/>.

73. Stafford, Jameson. Virgin America Flight Attendant Safety Dances to #VXsafetydance . 14 May 2014. 8 March 2015 <https://www.youtube.com/watch?v=r-eB-RPGezs/>.

74. Stafford, Jameson. Virgin America Flight Attendant Safety Dances to #VXsafetydance . 14 May 2014. 8 March 2015 <https://www.youtube.com/watch?v=r-eB-RPGezs/>.

## CHAPTER 6

75. Merrim-Webster . Pitfall. 2015. 8 March 2015 <http://www.merriam-webster.com/dictionary/pitfall/>.

76. Accenture. Promises, Promises: Easily Made, Easily Broken. How Keeping Your Promises Can Improve Customer Service, Brand Image and Loyalty. 14 August 2013. 8 March 2015 <http://www.accenture.com/us-en/Pages/insight-broken-promises-companies-retain-customers.aspx>.

77. Yarow, Jay. Here's How Amazon Can Get Away With Never Earning A Profit. 2 December 2014. 8 March 2015 <http://www.businessinsider.com/jeff-bezos-on-profits-2014-12#ixzz3TrPYU6Wf/>.

78. D., Dario. Ads vs. Reality – Fast Food. 20 August 2010. 8 March 2015 <http://www.alphaila.com/articles/failure/fast-food-false-advertising-vs-reality/>.

79. Herbert, Alastair and Ali Goode. Brand communication: Mind your brand language. May 2014. 8 March 2015 <http://www.warc.com/Content/Documents/A101755_Brand_communication_Mind_your_brand_language.content?PUB=ADMAP&CID=A101755&ID=357e143b-cfa3-4896-9ac2-481fe2462b57&q=&qr=>.

80. Lerman, Rachel. Starbucks launches huge roastery, restaurant, 'coffee theater' in Seattle's Capitol Hill. 4 December 2014. 8 March 2015 <http://www.bizjournals.com/seattle/blog/2014/12/starbucks-launches-huge-roastery-restaurantcoffee.html?page=all>.

81. Lerman, Rachel. Starbucks launches huge roastery, restaurant, 'coffee theater' in Seattle's Capitol Hill. 4 December 2014. 8 March 2015 <http://www.bizjournals.com/seattle/blog/2014/12/starbucks-launches-huge-roastery-restaurantcoffee.html?page=all>.

82. Mourdoukoutas, Panos. A Strategic Mistake That Haunts JC Penny. 27 September 2013. 8 March 2015 <http://www.forbes.com/sites/panosmourdoukoutas/2013/09/27/a-strategic-mistake-that-haunts-j-c-penney/>.

## CHAPTER 7

83. Flett, Chris V. Market Shark: How to be a Big Fish in a Small Pond. New York: Norseman Press, 2014. 153. Print.

84. Gobe, Marc. Emotional Branding: The New Paradigm for Connecting Brands to People. New York: Allworth Press, 2009. xxix. Print.

85. Jantsch, John. The Referral Engine: Teaching Your Business to Market Itself. New York: Portfolio/Penguin, 2012. 3. Print.

86. 3M. Who We Are. 2015. 8 March 2015 <http://solutions.3m.com/wps/portal/3M/en_US/3M-Company/Information/AboutUs/WhoWeAre/>.

87. 3M. Message to Employees and Suppliers. 2015. 8 March 2015 <http://solutions.3m.com/wps/portal/3M/en_WW/Corp/Identity/Strategies-Policies/Message/>.

88. 3M. Corporate & Brand Key Messages. 2015. 8 March 2015 <http://solutions.3m.com/wps/
portal/3M/en_WW/Corp/Identity/Strategies-Policies/Key-Messages/>.

89  Rose, Frank. The Art of Immersion: Why Do We Tell Stories? 8 March 2011. 8 March 2015
<http://www.wired.com/2011/03/why-do-we-tell-stories/all/>.

90. New York Times Insights. The Psychology of Sharing. 2015. 8 March 2015
<http://nytmarketing.whsites.net/mediakit/pos/>.

91. Murdoch, Jim. All alone in the blogiverse. 3 December 2014. 25 March 2015
<http://mcvoices.weebly.com/jim-murdochs-blog/all-alone-in-the-blogiverse/>.

## CHAPTER 8

92. Krug, Steve. Don't Make Me Think! A Common Sense Approach to Web Usability. 2nd. Berkeley:
New Riders, 2006. 11. Print.

## CHAPTER 9

None

# ACKNOWLEDGEMENTS

This book demonstrates the validity of one of my guiding principles: *Two heads are better than one*. I deeply appreciate the many people who contributed to the book's inception, construction and completion.

*Competition is Irrelevant* started when Chris Flett said to me, "You have a lot of good stuff in your head. Have you ever thought of writing a book?" Thanks to Chris for planting the seed, as well as supporting, encouraging and pushing me forward from the first outline to the book's publication.

Julia Ogburn, Marketing & Business Development Coordinator for *Marckworth Associates*, made things happen. Vital things—accomplished only because she made sure I did them or she did them herself. I benefit in so many ways from her skills, strengths and talents. The book would not exist without her.

Special thanks to Lois Stanford, my sister and invaluable editor. From the beginning she knew when to be my big sister and when to be a professional editor—she does both very well. She proved she was the ideal person for the job when, sitting at her dining room table editing the final manuscript, she said, "This is so fun!" Editing fun...? I thought she was kidding. She was not. I'm lucky.

Jeaneen Schmidt taught me the concept *Retreat to Advance*. We practiced this technique in scenic getaways across Puget Sound. She shared her Bainbridge Island home with me as a writer's retreat. Our friendship, deep conversations, good meals and long walks with my dog Tucker, contributed to every page.

I was fortunate to be a part of *Entourage*, a coaching group led by Jeaneen. Thanks to all the members of that group for their insight and support. Naomi Knight's and Nina Simonds' comments during the writing of the book had a common theme—*just keep writing*. Good advice.

Lynne Lazaroff, Julie Kalmus and Ted Kalmus read the first draft and offered me insightful and absolutely on-point comments. Those comments sent me grumbling back to the keyboard to revise and rewrite. Thanks to them the book gained strength and cohesiveness. I am grateful for the hours they spent, their suggestions and their friendship.

I benefit, along with many of my clients, from the outstanding graphic design of Leslie Waltzer *(www.crowfootdesign.com)*. She transformed my disjointed ramblings into graphic representations, resulting in a cover I love and a book I want to share.

I am deeply thankful for my friends and family who love and nurture me in so many ways. You know who you and how much you mean to me. I feel privileged to have all of you in my life.

My husband, Steve Felton, believes in me comprehensively, no matter how crazy my ideas. Quit my job and go to graduate school? Why not? Change career? Good idea. Start a business? Definitely. Write a book? Absolutely. I have spent my whole adult life with him and I am glad—every day.

My daughter, Amelia Marckworth, teaches me about myself and about life. During the writing of this book she helped me understand the concept of *productive procrastination*: doing seemingly random things that free your mind to work creatively. Writing this book included a lot of productive procrastination. Thanks to Amelia I realized this was okay.

My clients deserve a tremendous thank you. Every person I work with pushes me to know more and teach more effectively. I dedicate this book to each of you.

# ABOUT THE AUTHOR

Peg Marckworth is the principal of Marckworth Associates. She creates brands for companies, professionals and individuals that set them apart from the competition and catch the attention of the right clients. Peg has a 25+ year career in communications including co-ownership of an award-winning public relations firm, child welfare administrator, Washington State lobbyist and family therapist.

Peg's collaborative, strengths-focused approach is based on her ability to see the potential in others and build on their strengths. Peg's background in marketing, public relations and cognitive behavioral therapy gives her a unique perspective on people's strengths and how to highlight them. Her real world and theoretical understanding of individual and group change helps her clients succeed. Peg holds a Master of Social Work and a BA in Psychology.

Find more information about Marckworth Associates at www.marckworth.com

20069417R00109

Made in the USA
Middletown, DE
14 May 2015